Praise f

Living Grieving

"*Karen Johnson has written a guide to grieving that reads like a hero's journey tale. It is the story of her courageous and unlikely voyage from the life of a professional woman—a Fulbright scholar, a lawyer, and judge—who finds herself heartbroken and unmoored by the death of her son. Who she was before his death, and who she becomes because of his death, and her willingness to listen to the call of her son's spirit; inspired me, awakened me, and reminded me to continually choose a bigger life. Whatever your loss—a loved one, a job, a sense of self—you too will find her story and guidance profoundly helpful and transformational.*"

— **Elizabeth Lesser**, co-founder, Omega Institute and best-selling author of *Broken Open: How Difficult Times Can Help Us Grow*, *Cassandra Speaks*, and other books

"*The owner's manual for embracing grief with courage and transforming it into wisdom to discover the ultimate and lasting gift of joy.*"

— **Alberto Villoldo Ph.D.**, best-selling author of *Heart of the Shaman* and *One Spirit Medicine*

"*Comprehensive, cogent, and compelling. Through an empowering and thought-provoking narrative of her personal journey, fully supported by thorough research and acclaimed teachings in this field, Karen Johnson has gifted us with an extraordinary resource. This book provided me a unique and insightful roadmap to overcome the debilitating grief I was lost in for years after the death of my son.*"

— **Bobbie J. McCartney**, Chief Judge, USDA (Ret.)

"Karen's book is an important guide for these particular earth times. Might we all learn what she has learned. In times of great change, transforming loss into a life of personal meaning might be our most important contribution. Karen's journey gifts us a way to step with awareness into the river of love. She guides us through our sorrow in a unique journey of transformation, resurrection, and rebirth using profound quotes and powerful exercises to widen the banks and increase the depth of our love. This book is for every one of us who chose to be present during this cycle of great change. Thank goodness we have a loving guide. This book is a gift of sacrifice by a master shaman."

— **Nettie Jean Scarzafava**, Judge, Otsego County (Ret.)

Living
Grieving

Living Grieving

USING ENERGY MEDICINE TO ALCHEMIZE GRIEF AND LOSS

KAREN V. JOHNSON

HAY HOUSE, INC.
Carlsbad, California • New York City
London • Sydney • New Delhi

Published in the United States by: Hay House, Inc.: www.hayhouse.com®
Published in Australia by: Hay House Australia Pty. Ltd.: www.hayhouse
.com.au • **Published in the United Kingdom by:** Hay House UK, Ltd.: www
.hayhouse.co.uk • **Published in India by:** Hay House Publishers India: www
.hayhouse.co.in

Project editor: Melody Guy • *Cover design:* Jordan Wannemacher
Interior design: Nick C. Welch

**Cataloging-in-Publication Data is on file
at the Library of Congress**

Tradepaper ISBN: 978-1-4019-6344-6
E-book ISBN: 978-1-4019-6345-3
Audiobook ISBN: 978-1-4019-6359-0

10 9 8 7 6 5 4 3 2 1
1st edition, July 2021

Printed in the United States of America

For my son, Ben, who gave me the gift of a
second chance at Life, and for my daughter,
Caty, who encourages me to Shake my Rattle
and Release my Inner Butterfly

Contents

Foreword

When I first received the request to write this foreword, I had mixed feelings because of a full schedule of workshops and other projects with deadlines, yet something drew me to take a deeper look into the message of this book, and within a few moments of doing so I realized there were many synchronicities directing me to not only write this foreword but to go on a journey with the author, Karen. Today as I embark on the journey of writing the foreword, outside my window yellow butterflies are dancing, my rooster is crowing, and the pileated woodpecker is calling. I take all of these signs as a message of death and rebirth, which is very significant on this day because it is Easter, a holiday that is symbolic for the resurrection after the dark night of the soul.

There are so many places that I could begin. However, the best place to start is where I feel it most in my heart and that would be one of the first synchronicities, which is the passing of my soul mate and husband, Brad Collins, on August 2, 2014—three months to the day of the author's son, Ben, passing to the other side. After my husband's passing, I found myself on a similar journey as Karen and entered into a deep state of nonattachment that was quite different from my everyday busy life. I withdrew from teaching for almost a year. During that time, I experienced traveling around my own medicine wheel, which I actually have on my land here at my retreat in North Carolina. I decided to experience the nondoing, beginner's mind, and not live by time, schedules, or other people's expectations. This complete emptying out gave me the soft dark space of the void, creating a gentle place for me to come apart. After a time of no-thing-ness, when my heart and soul was ready, the wheel began to turn again bringing rebirth and love along with a deepening of my creativity and gifts to myself and the world.

Karen's teachings about her journey around the medicine wheel, beginning with becoming unstuck in the South, becoming lighter in the West, awakening in the North, and completing with creating a new life in the East, has many similarities to the medicine wheel and spiral path teachings that are not only integral parts of my own shamanic spiritual path, but also the core teachings of my Venus Rising programs. Throughout my own life I have passed through what I refer to as many shamanic initiations of death and rebirth. Sometimes this has been reflected by the passing of a dear loved one and at other times it has been more of an inner death of an old pattern, mindset, and way of being that no longer served my soul. This has required a constant return to humility and surrender to the spiral path around the medicine wheel of life again and again with each turn of the wheel. I remember a saying I once heard from the Sufis: "Oh when the great wheel of life turns, who can stand against it . . . certainly not I." There comes a time when something so big and earth shattering brings us to our knees and the only appropriate response is a humble one and to allow ourself, in Karen's words, to enter into the deconstruction process. My spiritual shamanic Wolf Clan grandmother, Twylah Nitsch, used to say to me, "If you know where you're goin' it ain't no place new." After a tragedy such as the untimely passing of a loved one, there is no going back to what was before and the sooner our egos can grasp that, the sooner we can begin to make the journey to becoming unstuck. Karen offers exercises to step onto the beauty way and begin the process of transformation in the South. She suggests dropping into fearlessness and nondoing to lighten our load, moving on to develop a beginner's mind and live in integrity as we resurrect our lives and complete the journey around the wheel using exercises and practices to rebirth our lives by owning our own projections and embracing indigenous alchemy.

I really enjoyed the author's embrace of what I often refer to in my teachings as the light, the dark, no difference. She does a beautiful job with speaking about grief and how it is a state of being that in time can bring you the energy to create a new life. She compares its opposite emotions—wonder, joy, and excitement—explaining that no one really talks about "the wondrous wisdom of grief" and rather than being supported by others we are often pressured to move past it as soon as possible and get back to normal. Karen's journey involves the continuation and beginning journey with her son, Ben, which enabled her to make radical changes in her life to make it more meaningful and bring her to a place of soul purpose and planetary service.

In this time of what feels like fast-food spirituality, it's refreshing to hear from a shamanic kindred sister who has undergone such a powerful journey so fully and has reemerged to reclaim her new life while sharing her wisdom and journey with the world. I want to thank Karen for inviting me to write the foreword for her book because it gave me the opportunity to not only learn more about the path of the medicine wheel but also to revisit, reflect, and experience the gratitude that my similar journey gave me. This journey created a place of rebirth that helped me to step into a beautiful new life beyond my own imagination. I want to also thank Karen for her courage not only to embark upon this journey, for it is not for the faint of heart, but to continue on it while sharing the wisdom she has gained from this death and rebirth experience. When we are open to it, our relationships with those who have passed through death's door can grow even richer and more beautiful. This brings a peace that passes all understanding as well as a deep revelation of the bigger picture for which is there is no end but constant cycles of death and rebirth along with the evolution of love and consciousness. Every death is a new beginning.

—Linda Star Wolf Ph.D., director and creator of Venus Rising Association for Transformation & University, and creator of the Shamanic Breathwork Journey process

Introduction

To my readers and fellow grievers:

I want you to know something really important. You may be feeling stuck in your grief and wondering why you can't seem to get over it. I felt the same way until I realized we do not get over grief. It's not like catching the flu; we aren't sick. There is no cure, and we can't medicate it away. Grief is a state of being that carries energy that you can tap into to create a new life. Just as we use the energy of other newly acquired states of being like marriage or parenthood to transform our lives, we can likewise use the energy of grieving to transform.

We don't see the possibilities in our grieving state because grief feels different. Unlike the emotions of wonder, joy, and excitement surrounding marriage and birth, grief is often associated with pain, sadness, and despair. We hear about and look forward to the wonders of marriage and the joys of parenthood, but no one talks about the wondrous wisdom of grief. So instead of embracing our grieving state and exploring its deep transformational wisdom, we just want to find a way to make the pain go away. And rather than being supported, we often are pressured from our loved ones and the medical community to get over it and move on. We are encouraged to seek therapy or take a pill to dull our senses. Grief is different because our pain makes those around us uncomfortable. The sooner we can get over it, the sooner things can get back to normal for everyone.

Before I experienced grieving for myself, it never occurred to me to see grief as a journey of transformation, or to find the blessings of the grieving process, or to allow myself to grow into the state of living with grief. I had to figure it out by myself. It was a lonely path of self-discovery that was not mainstream and not accepted.

I didn't bow to social expectation and "accept it" or "get over it" in a way that made people around me comfortable. Instead, I did the unexpected. I retired, sold my house and all my household goods, and went on a two-and-a-half-year journey that took me all over the world on a search for finding a way to go on living. In the beginning, I wasn't sure I even wanted to continue to live. But the journey ended up teaching me that my life after my son Ben's death was important and instructive to him and likewise that Ben's life after death was important and instructive to me. I learned, to my great surprise and comfort, that our journey together continued after his death. Undertaking a two-and-a-half-year odyssey to find answers was considered to be so far beyond the norm that my sanity was questioned by friends and acquaintances and even by myself. But I was fortunate: I had money and power, an unstoppable will, and a thirst to find meaning in my tragic loss and a way to honor my son's death.

My precious 27-year-old son, Ben, crossed over the rainbow bridge to the other side on November 2, 2014. He died of a heroin overdose. I never thought this could happen to him, to me, or to our family. I didn't see it coming; he wasn't an addict. The lives of those he left behind are forever changed by this tragedy. Death seemed completely final to me—it is death, after all. But I found there was so much more to death for Ben, and for me, when I realized we were both trying to figure out our new states of being. We both eventually found our way.

After Ben passed, I wanted to go after the drug dealers and the young man who sold him heroin. And I wanted to see the house and room where he died. The detective set up a visit to the house but instructed me to say nothing to the residents, including the "friend" who sold him the drugs. I know evidence was found that indicated the friend had delayed placing the emergency 911 call because he was hiding drug paraphernalia and flushing drugs down the toilet. Might Ben have lived if the 911 call had been placed immediately? Perhaps, if he'd received a dose of Narcan—an opioid-antagonist drug used to reverse overdoses—in time, he might have been saved.

Ben had taken $60 out of his bank account just before his death, and I found out afterward that a package of heroin sold for $10. I don't know if he was sold six packages or if all six packets were used. He was a big guy, so maybe he was given a large dose; all I know is that, in the U.S., life is cheap. You can die for $60—maybe even less. The heroin Ben used was pure and not cut with other drugs. The dose he was given was lethal, and the outcome for Ben was fatal.

The heroin epidemic in the U.S. is rampant. I recently read that more people in the country died from overdoses in 2017 than were killed during the Vietnam War. During the COVID pandemic, overdoses are increasing in every state and county in America at an alarming rate. A statistic from the Centers for Disease Control and Prevention, before the pandemic, showed that 116 people die every day in the U.S. from opioid-related overdoses. These numbers are huge and alarming. What the statistics don't show are all those left behind who are touched by the deaths. Mothers, fathers, sisters, brothers, aunts, uncles, cousins, and friends. All now entering new territory—the state of grieving—with little support or knowledge of this new terrain. So many cries of "Why us?" and "Please help me" that go unanswered.

Ben's death rocked the entire family—his father, sister, uncles, aunts, cousins, and grandparents. The cold fingers of death rippled out into the community of Ben's friends and acquaintances, his classmates, and all those who shared our lives. We all were forever singled out by death. We now belonged to a new category: those who have suffered great loss. I have heard it said that an unexpected death and the death of a child are the two most difficult losses to face. And if you have suffered the unexpected death of a child, you are in a very painful category indeed. But whether you were shocked out of your reality by the unexpected nature of death or whether it slipped away bit by bit as you help-lessly watched a loved one slide into addiction or become suicidal, you have been left standing on the shores of grief and despair. They are gone. We have been left behind. To cope, or not.

The truth is that "accepting it" and "getting over it" are clichés foisted on us to make those around us feel comfort-able. The truth is that we don't have to "accept it" or "get over it," but we can get through it. We can do more than pre-tend or medicate ourselves just to go through the motions of our lives. Lives that have been defined by Before Death Day and After Death Day. Our own special way of defining and measuring reality. I recently looked at books on Amazon and saw one I had ordered in June of 2014—I realized that I ordered that book four months before Ben's Death Day. At that moment in time, I had been ordering books and living a life that I had no idea would radically change in a few short months. I wondered what that woman, that me, was thinking about back then, what I was doing, what I should have done instead. If I had known then what was to come, maybe I wouldn't have ordered that book.

We, the bereaved, are sometimes changed by death in profound and, frankly, freaky ways. Let's have a conversation and open discussion around the secret subject of feeling and sensing and seeing our departed loved ones. Many of us, like me, keep this to ourselves out of fear. We think we won't be believed and that we might very well be sent off for therapy and medication. We think we will be mocked and talked about, minimalized and marginalized. So we keep this secret to ourselves, even from our spouses and children. Our secret contributes to our sense of isolation and despair; it keeps us stuck in the web of lifelessness. I offer my experiences of sensing and communicating with Ben to illuminate this gift that I felt I had to keep secret. I hope that by being open and vulnerable I can encourage dialogue about the wonderful ways we are given glimpses behind the veil of death. Glimpses that let us *know* that there is life after death. I *know* that Ben is happy. This is a treasure beyond measure; it helped me to find a new and meaningful life, and it can help you too.

I didn't think I could ever find my way out of despair, but I found a process that worked, a sacred journey and maps, and I want to share it with you so you can heal too. But make no mistake: this is not an easy journey. Instead of accepting death and the things we have been told about death such as, "It just happens," or "It is what it is," and "You have to accept it," I am proposing embracing death as a radical agent of change given to us out of *love*. Instead of the stagnation and despair that so often accompanies acceptance, embracing death through our journey allows us to ultimately bloom and grow into a new and better version of ourselves. Death has issued a challenge to us—we can seize the opportunity for growth or stagnate in despair. Our departed loved ones do not want to see us stagnate. They gave us the ultimate gift so we can create new and better lives. This is our destiny.

As an alternative to acceptance and stagnation, we can courageously make the journey through bereavement to transition, to resurrection, and, ultimately, to rebirth. There are maps in literature that can guide us, including the hero's journey, promoted in the work of Joseph Campbell. Another is found in the folktale of Paul Bunyan, the hero lumberjack, a story told through the eyes of Clay Filinger, a young man from the backwoods of Kentucky who leaves his home on an odyssey of American exploration. But this journey is our own—though we are guided by the map of the bereaved, each journey is sacred and unique.

Myths about death from cultures around the world connect the themes of transition, resurrection, and rebirth to the individual who has died. Transition marks the passage from one state to another. Our loved ones made their transition from the state of being alive in their physical bodies to the death of those bodies. Likewise, our lives have been changed from Before Death Day to After Death Day, and we have transitioned from a life that included our loved ones living with us in this physical plane to a place of deep and profound grief. A place where we can become stuck and bitter. Our loved ones then defy physical death and are awakened and resurrected in Spirit and then reborn to new spiritual lives, just as Christ in Christian mythology was resurrected and forever afterward associated with heaven, and as Osiris in Egyptian mythology was resurrected and associated with the underworld. We, too, the ones left behind, are on a sacred journey to awaken and resurrect our lives from this place of deep and profound grief, to be reborn into new lives.

I love the phrase "as above, so below" for the journey of the bereaved through transition, resurrection, and rebirth. We are mirroring the journey our loved ones are taking. Once I grasped that I, too, was on a journey, the pressure to get over it faded away. I could take my time and find my way through. Just like Ben, I could defy death by choosing a life with spiritual purpose. I could choose to live and love passionately and with great compassion, to forgive and be forgiven, and to become better rather than bitter, and then with great courage take the next step and be reborn into a new life of purpose and meaning from the ashes of the old.

How can we possibly do that, you might ask, with death sitting like an elephant in our hearts? We have been enculturated to believe we must ignore this elephant or toss it out on its ear. We must get rid of our grief. But that elephant is heavy and very stubborn, and not going anywhere by force. Instead we must befriend the grief in our heart and learn what it has to teach us about living.

This book is structured around practices that are part of the Four Winds medicine wheel as developed by Alberto Villoldo, Ph.D. The Four Winds medicine wheel combines native practices of North and South America along with four insights: The Way of the Hero, The Way of the Luminous Warrior, The Way of the Seer, and The Way of the Sage. Each insight has four practices associated with each direction of the medicine wheel. I have associated the practices of each insight with one step along the hero's journey of the bereaved through transition, resurrection, and rebirth. The practices of the four directions are as follows:

- South direction: Transition/Becoming unstuck:
  Nonjudgment
  Nonsuffering
  Nonattachment
  The beauty way

- West direction: Resurrection/Becoming lighter:
  Nondoing
  Nonengagement
  Certainty
  Fearlessness

- North direction: Resurrection/Awakening:
  Beginner's mind
  Living consequently
  Invisibility
  Integrity

- East direction: Rebirth/Creating a new life:
  No mind
  Mastery of time
  Owning your own projections
  Indigenous alchemy

At the end of each direction of the medicine wheel, I offer exercises related to each of the four practices. These exercises are important ways of self-reflection, awareness, and action designed to illuminate the path forward. I found these exercises to be deeply meaningful in my own journey through transformation (becoming unstuck), resurrection (awakening), and rebirth (creating a new life), and I hope you will too.

It's not possible to go back to the lives we lived before death struck and forever changed our reality. But we do not have to remain stuck in the overwhelming emotions of guilt, anger, and despair—a stagnant place of lifelessness. Instead I invite you to join me on a wild ride to a new and powerful self-realized life. One created from radical acceptance of the power of death to strike us with transformational lightning and electrify us with powerful energy to bloom and blossom.

CHAPTER ONE

The Deconstruction Process

ONE LOST BOY

Ben was three weeks overdue. He didn't want to be born. I believe he knew this life would be difficult and he put it off until the last moment. He was in crisis. No heartbeat—then a faint one—then an emergency C-section. He was blue. I was frantic, his father fainted, and Ben was rushed to the NICU. Maybe Ben knew how much we loved him; maybe he knew he had a big purpose in life. In any case, he lived.

Sixteen years later . . .

Ben wanted to play football his freshman year in high school. The physical showed something was wrong with his spine. He was diagnosed with a condition resembling a hunchback, which got worse every year. He was nicknamed Quasimodo by his "friends." In his senior year, Ben ended up having a 12-hour surgery to insert two 17-inch rods in his spine. He missed most of the school year and had to graduate from an alternative high school. He also had hammer toes that had to be straightened with rods. It was an experimental procedure that failed, and when the rods came out, he ended up with jointless, floppy toes. It could be that he had a mild case of Marfan syndrome, a genetic disorder affecting the connective tissue, often resulting in joint and spine issues and heart defects. Indeed, his autopsy showed an enlarged heart consistent with the rest of his symptoms.

He railed against me and his father, saying he was a freak of nature and should never have been born. Even dating was difficult for him—he believed he was deformed and was self-conscious about the long scar on his spine and his floppy toes. We tried so many things to minimize that scar—even an expensive and painful laser process. Trying to reason with him that he now had a straight back led to more angry exchanges. He refused to take off his shirt in public or wear sandals. What I only dimly realized was that the scar was not only on his back, but it was also on his soul.

The rods in his back kept him from joining the military—something he dearly wanted—which was very traumatic for him. His father and I were both in the military, as were his paternal grandparents and my father. He believed everyone but him would be buried in Arlington, and he was wild with disappointment and frustration, wishing he had never been born. He was filled with rage and refused to consider any other options than those denied him. He was out of control, and I was powerless to help him. He began drinking heavily when he found out about his spine at age 16. Beer seemed to flow freely in our neighborhood, with older siblings and friends buying for younger teens.

I dreaded the nights and spent years worrying instead of sleeping. When he was in his late teens and early twenties, there were parties in our house. Kids snuck in the back door to the basement and brought in alcohol. Night after night

I fell asleep early because I had to get up early and awakened to partying teenagers and the smell of cigarette smoke. I would go down and chase the kids out of the house and face all the anger—me against them and them against me. I was paralyzed with fear and shame and lack of sleep. I did not want this to take place in my home but felt powerless to make it stop. It was better to have him at home, right? Better to chase them all off in the middle of the night than have Ben go who knows where, right? He was often drunk and belligerent, but I knew he was in pain, and he knew that I knew. Sometimes he would break down and cry and ask, "Why me? What did I do to deserve this?"

His father recommended kicking Ben out. He recommended "tough love" and letting Ben hit rock bottom as a supposed cure for bad behavior. But I couldn't do it. Underneath all Ben's behaviors was a lot of pain and fear and insecurity. I could find that soft part of him, and we connected there most of the time. And he knew I would never abandon him. No matter what. He was my son, and I chose him over everything, including my marriage. And I believed that someday, someway, he would find his way and I would be there supporting and encouraging him.

Then, when Ben was 22, he found Primerica, a company that trained people to sell life insurance and securities. Each person was an independent, unsalaried entrepreneur. They were trained to reach out to families and friends, make cold calls, and knock on doors to make sales. He was told that if you didn't meet your quotas, you didn't deserve to go out and have fun. If you weren't making money, it was because you weren't trying hard enough, and you didn't reward yourself with a social life. And so he began to stay home alone every night. He stopped drinking and partying.

In the beginning, I was relieved to see him focused on learning the business instead of drinking. He seemed to have found some purpose for at least a year or so, making progress, and proud of passing exams and earning small amounts of money. After a while, his focus became more like obsession and a downward spiral into negativity and self-blame. I watched him work 12-hour days and then come home and write page after page of affirmations related to success and self-worth. He watched as others made money and went to conferences he wanted to go to but didn't quite make the required sales for.

Others around him had more success with sales. Some had large, supportive families whom they could tap into or communities or church groups. I was an only child of an only child and had few relatives, as did his father. We helped the best we could, but it wasn't enough. Ben finally gave up after four disappointing years.

Ben was depressed and defeated by his lack of success. He refused to go to college when he graduated high school, saying he wanted to be an entrepreneur. With his exceedingly high IQ, this was entirely possible. He was always very smart but never liked school, and he struggled with diagnosed attention deficit disorder. Formal education was always difficult for him. But after his business failure, he agreed to give college a try. He started out in a community college and was doing well in his classes, except for a required math course. He believed he was going to fail the class, and he was devasted because he would have to take it over, setting him back another year. He was 27 and felt he was already too old to be beginning college. And, he couldn't find any profession that interested him. Everything he wanted to do, like police force, military, homeland security, or border patrol, required a physical exam that he would fail because of the two rods in his back. And he knew it.

He began drinking heavily again after he left Primerica. This time going out to bars often until four in the morning with "friends." I entered into another painful year of watching him try to find a life. Night after night I prayed him home, waiting half-awake until I heard the garage door open. I was exhausted with fear and worry and dread. My life was spent taking care of him by providing a stable home and food and money. I wanted desperately for something good to come along for him, a girlfriend he wanted to impress or a job that caught his interest. But nothing positive came his way. Instead everything seemed to be spiraling downward. He was drinking and gaining weight and seemed defeated. What I didn't know was that he was experimenting with drugs.

I tried to distract myself from my panic and fear by dating —but he didn't like any of the men I brought home, and dating just took me away from him and I knew he needed me. Sometimes I would feel such deep panic that I would abruptly end a date and flee back home to make sure Ben was okay. I desperately wanted to find some happiness somewhere. I began seeing someone and decided to go on vacation with him for 10 days in South Korea, putting my fears on hold.

Before I went on vacation, Ben wanted to talk to me, but the discussion didn't go well. It was one of those times when something I said upset him and he stormed off. I wasn't as receptive as I could have been. I was tired and short-tempered at possibly the worst moment—possibly the moment when he might have been going to reach out about something important. Maybe he wanted to talk to me about experimenting with drugs. I'll never know. But the guilt of missing that conversation is crippling.

Before my vacation, I just went along on autopilot, putting patches on things where I could so we didn't keep bleeding, but knowing that underneath was a big fucking deep hole. I made his favorite dinners and I stayed in so he didn't come home to an empty house. I agreed to go to South Korea, but I hoped to have a big conversation once I returned. The voice inside told me that something was very wrong with Ben. I knew that addressing it would take uncomfortable conversations that would highlight and magnify our emotions—his and mine.

I was prepared for it to be ugly and messy, but the sheer magnitude of the pain and despair and disappointment in that big hole was just too scary to contemplate. I wondered if it would be better to open our Pandora's box of emotions or to just continue on each day as I had for years, ignoring the hole and hoping if we ignored it long enough, something really good would happen for Ben. Then a Band-Aid could be put over the hole and we could forget all those inconvenient and scary emotions ever existed. As if they didn't leave marks on our souls.

It's about denial: You train your mind away from the big dark hole and you spin yourself a web of lies to hide the pain. If you try hard enough, you can forget the hole exists for a while. Instead, you focus on what's going on day to day because it's impossible to remain bent under the weight of the situation all day, every day. The graveness and dreariness and burden of carrying it causes you to become rude and distant to keep others away and keep the inevitable questions about how your child is doing at bay. Maybe also to keep all the bragging about how wonderful their child is doing at a safe distance because the comparisons make you weak at the knees with worry. And envy. And shame.

Despite everything, Ben could still be funny and happy-go-lucky with the biggest smile in the world. He was strong and tall at six-eight and more than 280 pounds. He was the one his friends went to when they needed help moving or for any kind of favor. He always had a lot of friends and sleepovers and parties when he was young. We tried sending him off to camp a few times, but he either refused to go or begged to come home once he got there. He wanted to stay at home.

One time I asked him what he thought he wanted to do when he grew up, and he said, "Don't worry, Mom, I don't think I will be here very long." I couldn't hear this or understand it, so of course I said, "Don't be silly. You will live a long life, so you have to be prepared." But Ben knew something I didn't.

As far back as kindergarten, Ben was a daydreamer, and I remember a psychologist saying that Ben "danced to the beat of a different drum." I thought, *How is that helpful?* I didn't even know what to make of it. How do we get him to dance to the same drum as the other kids? It put me into a panic. What was I supposed to do and how would he make it in this very structured, unforgiving world? He also had a difficult time with sports. I remember bribing him with a book to get him to pay attention in Little League. Motivated to get the book, he went up to bat and hit a home run. He could read and play video games for hours, but anything that didn't interest him was almost impossible to force or cajole him into performing. Reason didn't work and depriving him of privileges didn't work. He could be as stubborn as a mule, and there were often yelling and pleading sessions.

We were always at our wits' end with him and schooling. If I had known then what I now know, I would have chosen other ways. I would have enjoyed him more and pressured him much less. But I didn't know, and I couldn't imagine how his life would play out. We put him in a private school with small classes for two years in junior high with the idea that it would help him concentrate. He hated that school, and we had major arguments about completing the work so he could pass each grade. He finally convinced us to put him back in public school. But he didn't do well there either and was on the verge of failing. We pulled him out and began homeschooling. Since he wasn't at all self-motivated, this turned into a disaster too. There were many more fights and conflicts about getting the work done.

After his surgery, Ben ended up going to an alternative school to get his GED because he missed so many days of regular school. His senior year he was alone and lonely—so many of his friends never visited, and it hurt. When he graduated, he refused to even consider college. For several years he bulked up and spent a lot of time in a gym. He worked at a GNC store and as a bouncer.

Our younger child by 20 months, Caty, was the easy one who took the expected path with little resistance. She was always on top of things at school and she didn't suffer from the same physical problems Ben had. How was it for her when so much protection and attention was focused on her brother?

She took Advanced Placement classes in high school and took a math course at the local college her senior year because she had already taken all the math classes her high school offered. She was in the band and the orchestra. She strategically determined in high school that there were too many flute players and decided she would play the bassoon so she could be first chair. And she made it and continued to be first chair in college. She got into her first-choice college with early admission.

She graduated with honors, was Phi Beta Kappa, then went to South Korea to teach English for a few years, and came back and decided to get an engineering degree. She lived at home to save money while she was in school. All in all, by any standard, she was an extreme success. Ben and Caty were very close as young children, but as they grew up, they grew apart. They ran with very different crowds and had entirely different life goals. They fought a lot, but then would laugh over silly things that happened. I guess they were just being siblings, something that as an only child I struggled to understand. I know that Caty wishes things had been easier between them.

His sister's successes were not lost on Ben. He often asked why he was the one to have learning and physical issues? Why did he have to get the hunchback? Why did he have attention deficit disorder? I know he envied his sister and felt we favored her. It wasn't easy to be in the position of celebrating the achievements of one child and having little to celebrate with the other. Ben's one wish when he had his Primerica business was to sell enough to win one of the trips so he could take me. He wanted to make me proud. He wanted so badly the success that eluded him. I wanted it for him too.

I believed I was in for the long haul—taking care of him forever because he was so broken inside and out. We both knew it wasn't good for him to live with me—something had to happen. And it did. He was funny and loving with me. He would come in the door bopping his head to death metal music and playing an air guitar just because he knew it totally cracked me up. I would say to him, "What a sweet song to sing to your mommy." And we both would laugh. In the very last voice mail I got from him, he said, "I don't know why I get so mad at you sometimes, but I want you to know you are the best mom anyone could ever have." Thank God and thank Ben for that voice message. It has kept me going.

Even with trepidations about going on vacation to South Korea and leaving Ben behind, I went. One afternoon in Korea I had a gloomy feeling that stayed with me. My phone rang and for some reason I was terrified. The person on the line hung up before I could answer but left a voice message. It was from a detective and I desperately returned the call. I was hysterical—afraid that Ben had maybe had an accident or had been caught drinking and driving.

I asked what happened, but the detective wanted to talk with me in person. I told him I was half a world away. I begged him to please tell me what happened. He hesitated and then said—"Ben is dead. He died of a heroin overdose." Everything went black. I said, "No way—Are you sure it's him? Are you sure he's dead?" While I sobbed, my companion went to work finding me the next flight out of Seoul, which, because of the time difference, was not until the next morning—more than 12 hours away and then a 10½ hour flight home. I couldn't get back for more than 24 hours.

I called my daughter, my ex-husband, and my closest gal pals—those were the hardest calls to make. I can still hear my daughter's screams and my ex-husband's shocked voice. He had the painful job of tracking down Ben's body and was told that he couldn't see him because he had been taken by the medical examiner to a morgue that wasn't open to families and visiting. I am still astonished by the cruelty of an administrative system that keeps a child's body away from grieving parents.

I somehow made it through that night and to the airport the next morning. While sitting at the gate, Ben appeared to me. He was standing right in front of me and smiling his big, happy smile. I frantically called my former husband and told him that I had seen Ben's vision in the airport and that he must be alive in the morgue and trying to get out of the freezer. I begged him to call the medical examiner's office and have them check. My desperation was so profound that the morgue technician took pity on us and told him, "I just went to check again myself. I'm sorry, but Ben is dead, and he is not trying to get out."

After a 10-hour flight, and more than 24 hours after talking to the detective, I finally made it home. Even though he was gone, I felt Ben around me every day. I know this sounds a bit hard to believe but I was swimming in the deep end of a pool of grief and I now know that I had been broken open and had awakened to the reality of life after death.

Before Ben passed, I was not at all religious, and if someone had asked me about life after death, I would have told them that I believed dead was dead and there was nothing more. But seeing and feeling Ben changed everything. Suddenly I was in unfamiliar territory and did not have any skills to understand what was happening.

My beloved daughter and her fiancé stayed with me for a few weeks. I know she was worried about me. One of my friends dropped everything and drove six hours to be with me when my plane arrived. That cold, dark week, I remember saying to several of Ben's friends that I wanted to die too. "It's not fair. You can't leave the mother like this. I want to overdose too." I wanted to know where to get heroin, but they wouldn't help me. They just cried with me.

I completely lost it at the funeral home. I had to see and touch Ben's cold body that had been refrigerated for several days. My ex-husband tried to keep me away, but I pummeled him with my fists and pushed him aside to get to Ben. I held my beloved son and touched his hand for the last time. He had a sheet covering the top of his head so we couldn't see the autopsy stitches. He was so cold, and he wasn't there. I couldn't face the room with the coffins or urns; I couldn't pick anything. I ran outside to escape and was almost run down by a woman backing out in the parking lot. I stood behind her car dazed and started laughing hysterically—I wondered if we could get a two-for-the-price-of-one special if I got run over in the funeral home parking lot. Ben and me, together forever.

My daughter took over the funeral planning and a dear friend of mine came to stay with me for a week and help out. I was an administrative law judge and had been one for 15 years. When I called the office to tell them what happened, the chief judge told me that I could have two hours off from work for my son's funeral. Even though I was numb, I found that to be rather shocking and grossly unfeeling, but I didn't question his decision. Another friend, who was the assistant chief judge, took up my cause with the personnel office, and they told her I could take a week of administrative leave. One week. It was a blessing and a relief. It never occurred to me to question whether I could go back to work after only a week. Work was a familiar refuge. Long days at work and a horrible commute held the promise of bringing routine back into my shattered life.

I don't remember much of that week except the funeral director calling to tell me that because Ben had been so tall he hadn't been able to "squash" him into one urn, so there was some of him left over. He also asked what he should do with the two 17-inch rods that were in Ben's back. I remember saying to him, "This is his mother you are talking to, you know!" I was horrified and retraumatized, but I managed to order a second smaller urn. I told him to do whatever with the rods—I didn't want them!

The funeral that Caty planned was beautiful and the auditorium was filled with people. But to me it all seemed maudlin and surreal. I couldn't entirely grasp that Ben was dead, and I looked around for him, hoping he would show up like he did in the airport. But he didn't. Caty had hired a violin player she heard about but had never heard play. The violin music the musician played was screechingly dreadful. Caty and I looked at each other in shock. I remember turning to her and saying that Ben must be laughing his ass off. Such a funny guy on this side of the rainbow bridge and the other. There was a moment when people made comments about Ben and I knew I was supposed to get up and say something, but I was unable to—I couldn't find a word to say. I sat and cried. I wanted to die. I hoped he would forgive me.

A GLIMPSE BEYOND DEATH

A few weeks later, after my friend and my daughter and her fiancé left, I was home alone and frequently found myself crying and screaming on the steps leading upstairs to my bedroom. In the weeks after his death, Ben did not come again to me in his human form as he had at the airport, but I felt his presence and felt him around me and beside me or touching my shoulder.

One day, I could not seem to get enough energy to walk upstairs. I lay on the steps screaming until I threw up; then threw up more until I threw up blood. I felt Ben frantically fluttering above me, trying to communicate, but I couldn't hear him.

As his presence became more frantic, I did the unthinkable in my logic-driven legal world. I went to Google and searched for mediums, not sure how far I might have to go to find one. To my surprise, not only did Google have a list of psychic mediums in Fairfax County, Virginia, where I lived, but there were pages of them. One medium in particular stood out to me. It seemed at the time that her picture was larger than the others, so I picked her. Several days later, when I went back to my search to find her phone number again, her picture was the same size as all the others. I didn't know it then, but this was the way I began to be guided by Spirit.

The medium didn't like working with families until three or four months had passed after a loved one died. But I convinced her it was an emergency, that I was seeing and feeling Ben trying to communicate, and that I was not doing at all well. I told her I wanted to die too and needed to know what Ben was trying to tell me.

I drove to her house with great trepidation. I really had no idea if she could communicate with Ben or even if this medium stuff was real. But I knew that I was seeing and feeling something, and I was willing to try anything. And I felt I knew Ben well enough that she wouldn't be able to fool me.

The medium was still a bit reluctant until I told her that Ben had just flown into her office and was standing right beside me. I asked her to please just tell me what he was saying because, even though I could sense him, I couldn't hear him. At that point in time, I had no knowledge of clairaudience, clairsentience, or clairvoyance, or hearing, sensing, or seeing messages from the spirit world. The medium asked me to sit and began to ask questions of Ben. It was fascinating. She translated for Ben in the beginning. He told me he did not want me to die and to suffer so much. He said he was watching over me and his father and sister and that we had to go on with our lives.

Watching the medium talking with Ben and giving me information from him in a speaking style that was so absolutely Ben was an amazing experience. I made a recording, and to this day, the messages to me and his sister and father ring completely true. Ben said it was an accident, that he didn't mean to die. It was "a bone-headed move on his part." He said he was so sorry and didn't mean to make me suffer. He was okay and he was with his grandfather and others. One hour with the medium wasn't enough. I wanted more. I wanted to talk to Ben every day. I had more questions. A lot more. The rather astonished medium suggested that I might have some intuitive abilities of my own—as very few of her clients could feel and see their departed loved ones.

In my lonely childhood, from the time I was four until eight, we lived far out in the country in a small ranch-style home. There weren't many children around and I was often on my own while my mother cleaned and cooked. I had an invisible friend named Debbie, who had the most beautiful sparkling white wings and who told me she was a fairy.

Debbie lived in the big apple tree in our yard. We played for hours, climbing the tree, playing tag, and generally having fun together. Another other-worldly companion told me he was a Native American chief. He seemed old with dark plaited hair with feathers and often appeared in the basement of my house. No one could see him but me, and he scared the crap out of me. I refused to go into the basement. Having invisible friends did not go over well with my mother. She told me not to ever mention them to anyone else or I would end up "in the loony bin." This was during the '50s, and state-run psychiatric institutions were fairly common. So, if one was deemed to be too far out there, then it was entirely possible to end up institutionalized.

I kept my invisible friends to myself and by the time I was in high school, they had disappeared. I pretty much forgot about them until well after I began seeing and sensing Ben. Those early experiences had been buried deep in my psyche. It would take the trauma of Ben's death and great courage to bring these past experiences to light.

After the medium mentioned that I might have psychic abilities, I took the suggestion to heart. A few weeks later, I began mediumship training. My medium became my instructor and mentor and introduced me to a holistic center near me that offered courses in spirit guides, healing, Reiki, crystals, and all things spiritual. I drank it all in thirstily and single-mindedly, desperate to communicate with Ben. I remember being shocked to find these interesting and very different kinds of resources and people all around me who were completely invisible to me before.

Over the next year, as I grappled with my grief, I also was opened up to a new world. I took every class possible and reconnected with my childhood experiences. In a spirit-guide training class, I once again became aware of the presence of Debbie and the chief and that those beings were still with me and always had been there, waiting to guide me and to bring specific qualities to my life. Debbie represented fun and freedom and the chief represented courage and fearlessness. These were qualities that were buried deep within me when I turned away from them and they disappeared from my awareness.

I chose not to seek help from a grief counselor or doctor because I believed a traditional therapist would have put me on medication to stop the visits from Ben. My mother's words about the "loony bin" still haunted me. I believed a therapist would think I was hallucinating or maybe even psychotic—extreme grief is listed in the Diagnostic and Statistical Manual of Mental Disorders (DSM), a handbook used by health care professionals in the United States and much of the world as the authoritative guide to the diagnosis of mental disorders. After all, I had been a respected member of conservative society, and this kind of behavior was considered unseemly and extreme. Not only that, but because I was regularly reviewed for a security clearance at my job, a mental illness diagnosis could put my judicial position in jeopardy.

I might have been in therapy for years, chasing society's elusive definition of sanity. Instead, I chose to follow my instincts, which were screaming to me to keep going, to find out more about the spirit world and everything related to understanding it better. Astrology, numerology, mediumship, crystals, Kabbalah, chanting, spirit guides, you name it. It was all new to me and extremely enticing. I was like a kid in a candy store—I wanted it all. But I had to be careful; I was still employed as a federal judge and I knew that these activities would be frowned upon.

After the first medium session, Ben was still around, but he no longer seemed frantic. He was more watchful, and it seemed like he felt a bit guilty but always available to me. All

I had to do was ask him to be with me. Sometimes I would call for him at night, sometimes out loud and sometimes just silently, from my mind. I could see him as a translucent spirit and feel him lie down in the bed beside me at night or feel his hand on my shoulder. As time went on, I could "hear" him. But the kind of hearing was both a knowing what he was communicating and also hearing words in my head.

Ben passed on November 2nd, and a week before Christmas, I persuaded my daughter that I was functional and that it was time for her and her fiancé to go home. I wanted to be alone. It was too difficult to have to pretend that I was okay, even with my daughter. She knew I had visited the medium and she was glad that it brought me some peace. She too received a message from Ben. He told her he was sorry that they fought and that he had been "such a butthead." She and her fiancé had plans to fly across the country to visit his parents for Christmas and New Year's. The tickets had been purchased before Ben's death—and I told them to go and that I would be fine.

I was fine—it was a relief to be alone in my house. I could cry without holding back, and I could lie on top of Ben's bed as long as I wanted. I had many days off over the holiday season; long, empty days that passed by in a gray fog. I managed to rouse myself on days in between weekends and holidays to get up and get dressed and find my way to my office. Ben stayed with me most of Christmas Day and my birthday, which is the day after Christmas. He was always there fluttering around and above me as I sobbed. I could feel him standing behind me with his hand on my shoulder.

Ben was not, however, my only spiritual visitor during those holiday weeks. I began to awaken to find a spirit or two at the foot of my bed or hanging out in the hallway outside my bedroom and following me downstairs as I got my morning coffee. I could see and sense them, and I knew they were trying frantically to talk to me. "Look," I told them, "it's no use. I can see you but I can't hear what you are saying. You should go visit one of the real mediums around here. Maybe they can help you." Some stayed around, some left, and new ones came to visit. It was creepy to wake up and find spirits in my bedroom, but oddly enough I wasn't terrified because Ben was around too. I felt they just wanted to be seen even if I couldn't help them.

One night, I sat up in my bed and looked around and saw a roomful of spirits. I pointed at my bedroom door and said, "Everyone out. This is it. No more spirits in my bedroom except Ben." The astonishing part was that they actually disappeared or kind of floated out! I thought to myself, *Wow, I actually have a say in this!* I thought of Ben's job as a bouncer. *Was he helping me get rid of the other spirits? Maybe he was a spiritual bouncer too!*

After a while I noticed that there were eight or nine spirits that seemed to hang around the house when Ben was there. I began to recognize them. I made another appointment with my medium friend and instructor, and asked for her insights. She asked them who they were, and she told me that they were all souls of young people who died suddenly. They told her that together with Ben they received training by more advanced souls and that part of their journey was to help their families through the grieving process.

She also said that since my life force was so low after Ben passed and I was at such great risk of suicide or death, Ben and his team were dispatched to be with me. My death as a result of Ben's was not part of my life journey, and they were there to help me through the grieving process and onto a newer, wiser path. When I asked her what this new path was, she shook her head and said she was told "all will be revealed along the way. It is not for her to know the unfolding before it's time." *Okay,* I thought, *great. A mystical mystery!* And yet it was comforting to know that I was being looked after. And it was deeply comforting to me to know that Ben was happy and had friends and spiritual mentors he enjoyed. I began to relax and not feel so completely overwhelmed.

A few months after Ben passed, a friend called me and left a hysterical message with the news her father had died from a heroin overdose. I felt Ben close by me at that moment and I knew that he was telling me he could help her father to cross over. I called her back and left a voice mail, saying, "Ben is here with me and is telling me that he is going to help your father to cross over." I didn't know exactly how I knew that information at that moment. I just knew, and that was the beginning of my "knowing." I was clairsentient. I began to trust this knowing and to take the next step of explaining to others what I knew. I thought I would hear his voice and hear sentences, but I just knew what Ben was saying, and I began to also know what other spirits were saying.

When my friend called me back, she was very serious and somewhat in shock. She said in the background of my message was a voice overlay saying, "This is Ben. I will help," and then a few more times saying, "This is Ben." I was elated for him and for me! I knew that he was finding his way on the other side and that he was learning to help others. Another of his friends, an alcoholic, almost died one night. He called me a few days later from the hospital and told me that right before he passed out, he heard Ben's voice saying, "Hang in there, man, I'm right here with you." He said it got him through.

Sometimes Ben's spirit was interested in adventure and experiencing some of this world through me. About a year and a half after Ben's death, I was in Costa Rica with my daughter and her fiancé and his parents. Everyone but me decided to go zip-lining. I decided to go up the mountain with them to experience the butterfly sanctuary and the wild forest, but I wasn't going to zip-line because of my artificial hip. It was a gorgeous ride in a jeep up the mountain, deep into the jungle with a river crossing. The top of the mountain was magnificent and the butterflies stunning. Our group was on the way to pay for the zip line and we were told that it involved not only a zip line but also a monkey swing and a rappel. Suddenly I felt Ben's presence strongly beside me and I had an overwhelming urge to go on the zip line! It was exhilarating, and at one point I found myself hanging upside down.

I knew it was not just me on this zip line, and I said to Ben, "Remember, I'm sixty-two—this body can't do everything you can do!" I could hear his laugh and his excitement all through the trip, over the monkey vine and rappelling to the ground at the end. I thought, *How I wish we had done this together when you were alive. I'm so sorry.* I heard him clearly say, "Mom, don't feel sad. You still don't get it. I'm right here having this experience with you just as much as if I were in my body, and even more so!" It was then that I realized that I had become clairaudient, able to hear spirits in addition to seeing and knowing. I knew that my skills in feeling, sensing, and seeing the other world were steadily increasing and I also knew that it was happening for a reason. I was to use these skills to help others like me who needed to receive messages from their loved ones in order to heal from grief. At that moment, I knew that Ben's death and my deep grief had a big purpose.

Is this all a fantasy of mine? Am I imagining things? Is this a projection of what I want to believe? Possibly. But how is it that others feel, see, and hear him too? How is it that I feel, see, hear other spirits? How is it that I can communicate messages for others? Several months after my first medium experience, I began to train and develop psychic abilities intensely for months. I learned to "see" a number someone was thinking of, and "see" a place they had walked that morning, and even "see" where someone had been killed and where they were buried. I learned to trust these skills, but I was still working as a judge and these two worlds were in conflict.

As my psychic abilities intensified, my life as a judge became more attenuated. I felt like an outsider looking in. The work no longer interested me. I couldn't relate to the people around me. All that interested me was my foray into the spiritual world, and I couldn't talk about that at work. I felt divided and fractured and didn't know what to do.

My medium friend referred me to an evolutionary astrologer whom she believed could help. Two hours with him completely changed my life. Paul told me lots of things that I didn't comprehend at that time. Like my soul had moved away from Pluto energy of shame and fear and blame into Neptune energy of the mystic and had chosen the mystic path. He told me a lot of other amazing and incomprehensible things about my soul's purpose and not only what I had come here to do but what I would be experiencing in the next year. I remembered wishing that the two-hour session could end soon because it gave me a headache. I was beyond confused.

My big takeaway from my reading was the astrologer telling me about another woman who had a reading like mine and became a shaman. I was astonished that someone could become a shaman since I believed shamanism disappeared centuries ago. After my reading I did what I did best—I googled it. Neo-shamanism and the Four Winds Society popped up, a school that taught neo-shamanism, ancient healing practices combined with cutting-edge methods in nutrition, biology, and neuroscience. I was fascinated and decided to call and get more information.

The next thing I knew, I was on a plane headed for Palm Springs, California, and then on to a retreat center for training with the Four Winds Society. I didn't realize at the time that my life would be forever changed and that I was embarking on a new life path that would bring me purpose. Looking back at the reading from Paul a year later, I was struck by how he had predicted my life unfolding. Even though I didn't understand much of what he said, I heard the word *shaman* and it opened the door to the future.

What is a shaman? The word itself comes from a Siberian word meaning one who "sees" or "penetrates the source." Shamans and shamanic practices are ancient in origin and found around the world. Shamans in indigenous societies are often leaders in their communities. Shamans are also called healers, medicine men or women, and walkers between worlds. I like the image of "walkers between worlds" because that is what we do: we dance between the world of energy and the world of matter. We learn to enter into altered states through techniques like journeying, where we enter into special states of consciousness that are very different from our ordinary consciousness. Journeying allows us to access worlds beyond this one to gather information and assist ourselves and our clients to heal. Since I was already experiencing seeing beyond this world, shamanism seemed to be a natural fit for me.

Shamanism is linked to healing modalities and practice in the medicine wheel. The medicine wheel is an ancient symbol, depicting a circle or spiral, which is a metaphor for the interconnection and continuity of life. In this book we will explore the four cardinal directions of the Four Winds medicine wheel and the practices that are associated with each direction.

We will begin with the South direction, or serpent path, where we energetically shed our past and transform our deepest grief into sources of compassion and healing. We then move to the West, or jaguar path, where we will step beyond fear and death and connect with life. Next, we move to the North direction, or hummingbird path, where we learn to take a quantum leap outside of time and be resurrected into new and meaningful paths. Finally, in the East direction, or condor path, we are reborn and claim our new vision and step into who we are becoming beyond the confines of despair and learn to incorporate grief into a new life.

Death changes us. There is no way to be the person you were Before Death Day. Even though you did not ask to change and would do anything to turn back the clock, the person you were before is forever gone. Death visited your loved one and offered a new, bigger, and better life across the rainbow bridge to their After Death Day life. They had the courage to break free of the structures of their old life and say yes to a new life. I know this might sound strange, but I do believe that death was a choice for Ben and that he courageously chose to walk out of this life into the next. Death visited you too and is offering you a new, bigger, and better life. Will you break free of the familiar structures of stagnation and despair to find your way to your After Death Day life? Read on to discover more about the path that awaits you.

CHAPTER TWO

South Practices
of the
Medicine Wheel

Becoming Unstuck

In the South direction of the medicine wheel, we are on the path of the hero, turning our wounds and our stories into sources of power and compassion. The image of the serpent continually shedding its skin is used as a metaphor for our lives.

We can be stuck in our grieving because of disempowering stories starring us or others in tragic roles. Stories that we tell ourselves about how things might have ended up differently. These stories are diversions from confronting deep pain, sadness, and loss. If we take away the stories, we might be left with pain we cannot bear. But our stories are based on shame, blame, and guilt, all of which are anger turned inward and which cause us unnecessary suffering. By releasing anger we stop punishing ourselves or those around us, and then we can gain access to what is real: the pain of our loss.

When I began examining my own stories, I felt what I imagined a serpent might feel—hesitating to rub its old, crusty protective layer off and expose new and excruciatingly sensitive skin to the elements. Would I be able to look deeply at Ben's death and all that led up to it? Could I learn to forgive everyone and everything? Even myself, and even Ben? Could I once again find beauty around me? Could I transform my deep grief into a source of compassion and transformation?

It seemed auspicious to me that three of the practices of the South direction are nonsuffering, nonattachment, and nonjudgment. My life was a revolving door, swinging between attachment, judging, and suffering. They summed up my existence. The last practice, the beauty way, was one I was unfamiliar with and had to grow into!

As you read along with my story, you might find that you have reflections on your own stories that you want to jot down. At the end of this chapter there will be exercises designed to help you work through each of the four practices so you might begin your own journey through the transformation process.

NONJUDGMENT

When you go out into the woods and you look at trees, you see all these different trees. And some of them are bent, and some of them are straight, and some of them are evergreens, and some of them are whatever. And you look at the tree and you allow it. You see why it is the way it is. You sort of understand that it didn't get enough light, and so it turned that way. And you don't get all emotional about it. You just allow it. You appreciate the tree. The minute you get near humans, you lose all that. And you are constantly saying "you're too

this, or I'm too this." That judging mind comes in. And so I
practice turning people into trees. Which means appreciating
them just the way they are.

— RAM DASS

To practice nonjudgment we must give up our beliefs
about right or wrong and even our own opinions. Our opinions are based on strongly held beliefs we have absorbed
from our experiences and culture. We observe everyone and
everything around us through the lens of what we think we
know. But what if what we think we know is keeping us from
growing and changing? What if we could see the people and
circumstances of our lives in a new and different way?

How does one even begin the process of attaining nonjudgment when one starts off with the job of federal judge?
Seriously. In my law-ruled world things were either black
or white or gray with the caveat that all gray things could,
should, must be turned into black or white things. Would I
be able to let go of my beliefs and the stories around them?
Would letting go allow me to even let go of the trauma stories around Ben's death?

When I called the Four Winds office, I wasn't sure I was
going to sign up; I just wanted to talk and see what it was all
about. The website was beautiful and all the classes looked
very exotic and interesting. There were even trips to Peru.
Trips are good, right? We talked for an hour and a half. At
the end I gave my new academic advisor my credit card and
signed up for the one-week South direction class.

Three weeks later I found myself on a plane to Joshua
Tree Retreat Center in California for a class on the first part
of the medicine wheel. It was a big secret. I told no one
except my closest of friends. I told my office and anyone who

asked that I was going on a vacation to California. I certainly deserved a vacation, so no one asked a lot of questions. The few friends I told thought I was crazy and grief-ridden but were happy to see me doing something, anything, to get me out of the house and my self-imposed isolation.

On the plane I berated myself for being a suggestible fool. I would probably be too old for the class and I would stick out, like a sore thumb, from all the eccentrics I was sure to meet. Moreover, I already felt cut off from my familiar job and taking classes in shamanism was likely to pull me even further away from all I knew into more uncertainty. I considered canceling when I arrived, spending the night in Palm Springs at a resort and flying home the next day. A resort with nice beds and maybe a pool and a spa, a massage, and a facial sounded comfortingly sane and more like what my friends thought I needed. Instead I decided to at least take a look at the place. I could always check in and check right back out. After all, nobody knew me there and, more importantly, I wouldn't know anyone. For once I was completely on my own with no one to please and no responsibilities. I could leave. No questions asked.

And I was free of the constant and excruciating anxiety that I felt every time I left Ben to go on vacations before his death. But Ben was free and so was I. I could travel without fear or worry in the back of my mind. But I had exchanged it for grief, guilt, and despair. A trade I would never willingly have made.

I arrived at the retreat center after a long ride through the desert from Palm Springs International Airport. It looked like it was going to be very hot and dusty, and very remote. And it was. I registered, looking at the others and wondering if they would be classmates. I made sure I had a single room so I wouldn't get a roommate I might not like. And, also, so I could get away and isolate myself.

Isolation is a pattern in my life. I was born an only child of a father who was also an only child, and I grew up feeling very alone. I told myself it was better that way. Most people turned out to be a big disappointment anyway. The only reprieve was with the small family I created when I was married with two children. It was a wonderful interlude in my life, although it was challenging, and it often left me longing for the alone time I was accustomed to that wasn't possible while raising a family. Well, I ended up being a divorced empty nester and grieving mother. I had lots of alone time.

What happened in the South class? For one thing, I stayed, and for another I loved it! I wasn't the oldest nor the only one coming from a conservative background. There were doctors and lawyers, nurses, massage therapists, yoga instructors—a mix of everything in a class of 43 people, some very young and some, to my delight, older than me.

Just looking around the class that first day, I judged which students I might want to sit beside and which ones not so much. This one over here I wasn't sure I liked the looks of and that one over there I was sure was scowling at me. I had so much to learn. By the end of the week my smug confidence in my usual judgmental observations had been shattered as I was forced to interact with classmates not according to my choice but by what was referred to as the "spirit lottery." We chose slips of paper with numbers written on them and your partner was the one with the matching number. By the end of that week I became close to a variety of people I would never have chosen in the beginning, learning that what was underneath the mask of how someone looked, acted, and dressed was someone just like me. Just like me, they all had a story, and just like me, they were looking for a way to end their suffering and find meaning in life. Just like me, they were trees that had twisted and turned to try to find the light.

This revelation forever changed my perception of people. We learn to judge each other so harshly and so easily on the basis of mere seconds of observing the way someone looks or acts. Malcolm Gladwell, in *Blink: The Power of Thinking Without Thinking*, reveals how great decision makers have perfected the art of "thin-slicing"—filtering out and acting on the variables that matter. This is instinctual and survival based; our very safety turns on quick judgments and reactions.

There are predators and dangers lurking in our streets and even in our own homes and families. I know this to be true. Some of them sold the heroin that killed my son. But what if we are wrong? What if the factors we use to be successful in business and with like-minded people don't work as well when we are thrown out of our comfort zone? It took a long time for me to see a twisted tree of a person and allow them to just be. To really see and feel in my heart the lack of light that brought that tree to that moment. And to release the desire to want to do violence to it in return, to no longer want to grind it into sawdust. To see the twisted trunk and see it reaching for the light. In the end I realized one twisted tree was me and I had been doing great violence to myself for years.

In a quirk of my very human nature, I found it hardest to see relatives, friends, and neighbors who had been unkind to Ben or to me in the same way. They had wounded us deeply and I found it difficult to allow them to become trees. I clung to those wounds and ruminated about all the stories I wove around the wounds. Stories casting each person, including me, as wrong or bad, mean or hateful. As I reviewed and embellished the stories, they became bigger and more powerful and fueled the anger and pain that was deep within me. It has taken time and practice to allow all those who wounded me so deeply to be seen as trees, often very twisted ones, just trying to reach for the light, and not judge them. It took even more time and practice to see myself as a tree just trying to reach for the light in my own imperfect way. This practice has given me what some people call grace or inner peace.

All I know for sure is letting go of the urges to get even and say the mean things to settle old scores is freeing. I no longer spend time creating scenarios and the words and actions to go with them. And freedom allows my body to relax and sleep in peace. And I believe and know in my heart that it brings Ben peace as well. When I am frantic, I feel his spirit trying to calm mine. Instead I give him the gift of my peace. Looking back at my South class, I am grateful for the spirit lottery that allowed me to see and be seen by people whom I would never have known. It has opened my very narrow existence to friendships all over the world and to a life beyond what I could have imagined.

NONSUFFERING

Pain is inevitable. Suffering is optional.

— UNKNOWN

No mud, no lotus.

— THICH NHAT HANH

As I progressed in my journey, I pondered these two statements, which seemed to be at odds with one another, determined to reconcile their wisdom. The first, "Suffering is optional," seemed to me to lack compassion. The second, "No mud, no lotus," seemed full of compassion but lacking instruction about how to get to the lotus. As I looked deeply into Thich Nhat Hanh's teachings around suffering, I found the answer. The meaning behind "No mud, no lotus" is not only that we find the happiness of the lotus by suffering through the mud but also that when we know how to suffer, we suffer less. In my South direction class I learned about suffering and that in order to suffer less we must let go of the stories that we spin around the facts.

The fact is that my dear 27-year-old son died unexpectedly from a heroin overdose. But that mere fact ignited in me a quest to figure out not only what happened but why it happened. In my pain, it seemed to me that it must have happened because I had failed him as a mother. I spent a lot of time and anguish ruminating about the past and creating stories where I was the doomed star of the play, always at fault and always ultimately responsible for the tragic outcome. If only I had done things differently, all would have been well. I creatively invented stories going back to his birth, and the overwhelming guilt in those stories brought me to my knees in tears.

I mastered the guilt, shame, and blame trilogy early in life. Nothing I did seemed to please my mother and father and I was constantly criticized. I wasn't pretty enough, or thin enough, or smart enough. I was supposed to make my mother happy and I didn't succeed. Rather, she often told me that having me ruined her life. I believed that I was unworthy and did not deserve happiness.

I managed to find men and relationships that confirmed my feelings of worthlessness. I believed the only things I was good at were work and school, so I ended up with two master's degrees, a Fulbright scholarship, and a law degree, and then worked fiendishly and single-mindedly all my life to achieve and grab every brass ring of success offered. I tried hard to be a diligent worker and a perfect mother and felt great guilt as my efforts to do both seemed to be fraught with disappointment and failure. Being a diligent worker took a terrible toll on being a perfect mother or at least on what I imagined a perfect mother to be. I was often stressed out and exhausted.

My ultimate failure was losing Ben. Other families and other mothers did not face such a terrible loss. Other mothers were better. I could tell I was being judged by other parents. "She worked too much." "She was too permissive." "She bought her children too many things." "It's her fault." And I believed it and found my thoughts ruminating around these themes: If only I had done things differently. If only I had chosen differently Ben might be alive. If only I wasn't such a fuckup. If only I could die too.

These guilty thoughts caused me immense suffering. For the first two years after Ben died, I became a recluse except for my shaman and mediumship training. I refused almost all invitations, even from close friends. I told them that I had a broken heart and to think of me as half dead, like a zombie—and zombies don't go to lunch or movies or parties. Zombies stay away from the living and stay home by themselves, eating peanut butter and jelly because they can't even face going to the grocery store and seeing the foods they used to prepare for their loved one because that causes an unbearable memory and a stab of pain in the heart.

For me the isolation was intense and so was my guilt. I believed that if only I had not been in South Korea, I could have changed the outcome. If only I had not gone on vacation, if only I had listened more or been a better parent, this wouldn't have happened. And the guilt was intensified because I saw all around me the friends and colleagues and acquaintances who had sons who were struggling with addictions but lived through their crises.

Only later did I receive an answer to this question from a wise sister shaman. She said, "Really, it's very simple: the reason you had to leave and go on vacation was to give Ben the space to do what he needed to do." Yet again, Ben knew something I didn't know. He was ready to transition from this world to the next. These are not words that I wanted to hear or was ready to hear. Nor did I want to hear, even from Ben, that he was happy and doing great on the other side. Sometimes I was furious with him—how could he do this to me? I gave up everything for him, I supported him financially and emotionally. How could he leave me?

"Why me?" I asked. "Why did my son have to die?" It must be because I was bad, at fault, undeserving. This tragedy struck my family because I was flawed. I was so sunk in misery and guilt that I could not see the basic flaw in my thinking: imagining that I somehow had control over Ben's life. I believed that my running faster, jumping higher, and being a more perfect parent was the cause and effect of every decision he made—good or bad. No philosophical view was comforting. I heard that "Bad things happen to good people" and "It's not your fault." But the underlying premise—that I was a good person—was at the root of everything. I didn't believe that I was a good person or a good parent or a good mother. All I could see were the times I wasn't so good and the things I did or said that I wanted so badly to go back and change, and thereby change the awful outcome. I still wanted to believe that I was in control.

I wanted answers to questions like "Why did Ben pass so young?" "Why not me instead?" "Why my son?" "What was I supposed to do with myself now?" I found myself unable to concentrate on work or write or think. I managed to stumble into work each day out of habit and out of fear of the lonely, empty days when I was home alone. It was obvious I was a wreck, and everyone knew it. I remember sitting at a meeting my first week back and trying desperately not to sob. I knew it would be unseemly and make everyone uncomfortable. I held it in with great effort, my face turning red and my eyes beginning to water. I was the first who left the meeting, running to my office to shut the door and bawl.

I became unglued, lost my center, and went nutso. Don't get me wrong—I had lots of support from my daughter and her fiancé, and all my great gal pals. But the truth of it is that no one can guide someone through something like this. It is a solo journey.

Early on, the blame and guilt I tortured myself with resulted in my becoming suicidal. Christmas came exactly 53 days after Ben passed, and my 61st birthday was the day after Christmas. I wanted nothing to do with any of it, no decorations, and certainly no music about a son being born. I turned Ben's room into a shrine—nothing had been touched, not even his dirty clothes in the hamper and on the floor. I went to his room on and off every few hours to smell his scent and to talk with him and tell him how much I had loved him while he was here and how much I loved him still. I dozed for hours lying on his still unmade bed.

Days came and went and suddenly it was New Year's Eve. As I was lying in bed that night, the thought came to me that my life was complete and that I would be dead by morning. I believed angels had taken pity on me and would relieve my suffering by letting me die. The thought filled me with peace and longing to be with Ben. Much to my surprise, I woke up New Year's Day. I was alive and I felt betrayed; the classic bait and switch had been pulled on me by the universe! I was furious. I was not afraid of death—I welcomed it and even death had found me to be unworthy.

As that long, cold day progressed, I became possessed by the idea that I had to make 16 bundles of food, Ben's clothing, and his bedding for homeless people who had created a tent city under a railway trestle bridge near Union Station and my office. I had no idea why it had to be 16 bundles.

Since so many homeless people came and went, there was no way to predict how many would be there. But 16 seemed to be a good number, and it didn't occur to me to question it. I pulled out all the sheets and bedding that I had used for Ben and made 16 piles. Then I had the idea of adding Ben's clean T-shirts and socks to the pile. I added cookies, water, juice, and $10 to each. I folded up each bundle, tied them with Christmas ribbon and packed my car from top to bottom with them.

My small car was packed to the brim. I couldn't see out of the back windows, and even the passenger seat was stuffed full. I wondered if I could manage to drive the 25 miles to the homeless tent city without being stopped by the police, and what to say if I were stopped. I made it without incident, a bit anxious about whether I would have enough bundles to give one to each person there. I pulled up to the curb and counted the tents—there were exactly 16. I was touched, and even in my state of despair, I realized that this was a divine message instigated on my behalf by Ben. He was always so generous with his time and his belongings so his orchestrating the giving of his things to the homeless was perfect for him, and it was another way of reminding me that he was with me.

Three weeks later, my daughter went to Guatemala as a volunteer with the World Engineering Organization to fix medical equipment. After she left, I found out that my furnace was not only not working but it was also dangerously leaking carbon dioxide and needed to be replaced immediately. It occurred to me that this could be my way out—I could just die peacefully with my little dog, Murphy. To my deranged mind it looked like a perfectly logical solution. My death would look like an accident, and therefore my daughter wouldn't think that I took my own life and that she wasn't worth living for. Every morning for the three weeks she was away I woke up surprised to still be alive. When my daughter was on her way home, I replaced the leaky furnace and realized that instead of planning on dying, I needed to figure out how to live again.

But I didn't know how to go on living with the amount of guilt I was carrying around with me. In an effort to bring me comfort, someone told me our souls (mine and Ben's) had agreed to this ahead of time. Ben would pass early and that I would be here to support him as he worked out his karma. I was told that Ben was on his second to last incarnation and that he chose me as his mother to support him through all his difficulties (physical and emotional) in this lifetime. Also, I would get set on a spiritual path as a result of his sacrifice. This comforted me for a while; then I had a panic attack. I imagined us sitting at some kind of crazy cosmic tea party and agreeing that this big amount of loss and pain would be just ducky for the both of us to progress along our spiritual paths.

I thought what a horrible soul I must be to agree to let my son die young so I could find my spiritual path. Even more disturbing, I wondered what horrible, terrible agreements I had made with my beloved daughter. I shivered and thought, *What's coming next?* I was bruised and broken and utterly hopeless. I had the sensation of being a magician's assistant, floating in the air, unmoving, my hair hanging, neither on earth nor in heaven. Dangling in between. Helpless.

This was my point of complete deconstruction. I had fallen into a pit so deep and so dark I did not believe there was a way out or that I deserved to get out. I was convinced that the level of my suffering and my guilt and sadness demonstrated my level of caring and profound, breathtaking loss. And that I would never forget Ben.

At some level I knew that the stories I was creating were causing myself more suffering, but at another level I believed

I deserved to suffer because I was to blame. All I wanted was to be alone. Aloneness held out the promise of less suffering because no one asked how things were going or looked at me with sadness or pity in their eyes. I tried desperately to keep the Band-Aid of avoidance firmly in place, as I thought ripping it off would bring all the pain back to the surface. Mostly, it was surprisingly easy to do—most people wanted to avoid talking about Ben's death at all costs and would go to great lengths to talk about anything else. Nobody wants to look grief in the face; nobody wants to see you cry.

But suffering ate away at me mentally, physically, and spiritually, and remained boiling beneath the surface, infecting everything in a deeply dark and intensely negative way, like a pot left boiling on the stove until nothing is left but a sticky burned mess at the bottom because the heat caused all of the light and beauty and goodness to boil away.

I knew I had to let go of all these stories, but I didn't know how. They had become a part of me, and I clung to my suffering. I visited a shaman pal in Taos, New Mexico. She has land and a retreat center beside an Indian ashram and temple with an incarnation of Hanuman, the monkey god. I had never been near an ashram before. As I neared the temple, I began to weep uncontrollably, and I continued to weep as we entered the shrine room—big, loud sobs that I couldn't suppress, tears and snot pouring like a river from my nose and eyes. I didn't even have a tissue and all I could do was wipe my face on my sleeve. I might have been embarrassed except I was tuned in to a male Indian voice that only I could hear, saying to me clearly, "You must work on self-love. Your son's death is not your fault." I knew in my heart that Hanuman was speaking to me and the diety's words touched my aching heart. Self-love had never been part of my lexicon. How might it be to focus on self-love instead of shame, blame, and guilt? What if Ben's death was not my fault? What then? What would become of all the old stories?

Letting go of the stories featuring shame, blame, and guilt was a process. I had to look at each belief, each memory, and each action and ask myself whether it was true that I had control. Was it true that I caused Ben's pain? Was it true that I had the power to make Ben's choices for him? And finally, was it true that my suffering demonstrated to Ben or to myself or to anyone else the level of my caring or the depth of my love and loss?

All I know for sure is that as I released the stories and my suffering lessened, as my mind cleared, and as the veils of darkness dissipated, I could see and feel and remember all the loving memories that had been cloaked as I punished myself beneath suffering's dark shroud. As I stopped punishing myself, my heart opened to the wonders of self-love, something missing in my life for a very long time.

NONATTACHMENT

If we fearfully cling
To what we have,
We will never be able to discover
Who we truly are.

— SRI CHINMOY

The practice of nonattachment involves letting go of the roles that we have created for ourselves and the ones that others have created for us. It also involves letting go of the possessions and lifestyles associated with these roles. These roles have become so much a part of us that they have come to define us. And what defines us also confines us. For me, every time I put on my judicial robe and stepped out of my office, I became a different person. I became *the Judge*. Even when I didn't have my robe on, people would greet me, "Hi, judge." Even when I was doing a bit of gardening at home, a neighbor looked at me and said, "I didn't know judges did gardening!" It was a very heavy role that followed me. I remember talking with a Jesuit priest in an airport. I asked him how it felt to wear his cassock everywhere. I, at least, could take my robe off and go incognito. He told me that being a priest and wearing a cassock is so much a part of him that he could not imagine going out into the world otherwise. So, letting go of roles has everything to do with letting go of our identification with these roles so we can imagine going out into the world in a different way.

When Ben died, I fell deeply into the role of the grieving mother. It became my new identity. I could not even imagine shedding this role—it seemed to me that if I did, I would be shedding Ben and that I was not prepared to do. The role of the grieving mother was linked to feelings of hopelessness and despair that kept me feeling frozen and trapped in ice. I was also deeply attached to being a mother to my daughter. I couldn't imagine letting go of that role either, and I wasn't sure I wanted to.

My lifestyle, home, and possessions I believed demonstrated my achievements: I had worked hard to become a lawyer and then a judge, and my home and my lifestyle reflected success, and I couldn't imagine a different life or way of being. I had bought into the confines of my lifestyle and just doing something out of the ordinary, like attending mediumship classes and going to shaman school, put me into a panic. What if I was found out? What would happen? I could be fired or the subject of a *Washington Post* article—I would be a laughingstock! It was terrifying.

If people looked at my life before Ben passed, they would have said, "I want what she has: two beautiful children; a high-paying, powerful job with lifetime job security; a beautiful five-bedroom, five-bathroom house in a community with a pool and tennis court; expensive cars; a successful husband; and successful and important friends and acquaintances." I got accolades for using my brains for learning and achieving, making money, and marrying and having children. We are not rewarded for turning our backs on the American dream—in fact it's pretty darn hard to disconnect.

It was springtime in D.C., about a year and a half after Ben's death. And there were three planets in retrograde. I was told by my newfound spiritual friends that this accounted for finding myself paralyzed emotionally, physically in pain, and exhausted. None of the trappings of success had meaning anymore. My logical, analytical mind had abandoned me. My house was too big and empty and lonely and filled with unbearable memories of the past.

I was increasingly unhappy with driving twice a day in the second-worst traffic in the country and with long days at a boring, meaningless job. I began to see my routines as soul-crushing. Year after year of cases to decide and decisions to write, walking the same hallways, lunching at the same restaurants, leaving the house in the dark to sit for more than an hour in heavy traffic that crawled at 20 miles per hour, then sit for long days in court or in my office, then sit in my car again in more slow traffic to go home in the dark. I wondered how I was able to continue these routines for so many years without examining them. But I had numbed myself in order to survive and keep going. I dared not examine my life because if I looked really hard, I would see that I was miserable and that would lead to big changes.

Ben's passing was the catalyst that threw me out of all that was familiar to me and allowed me to make those big changes. I simply couldn't fit myself back into my old life. I knew that I wanted something more from life. I wanted to live outside of my self-imposed constraints as well as the constraints that I had bought into willingly. I wanted desperately to heal this big aching ball of pain, but I couldn't seem to figure out how. I had a feeling that healing would involve letting go of all these familiar things, but then what?

I had been practicing law for more than 30 years, and I had been a judge for 13 of those years. I was now 62, and it seemed to my mind that it was late in life to be making massive changes. During the 30-odd years that I practiced law, I had also married, raised a family, and cared for my elderly parents. Many of those years I was in the so-called sandwich of being squeezed by the caretaking of children and parents. There was little time during those years for self-reflection or self-care. I really don't remember much of my 40s at all—it's a blur of doing and going and exhaustion coated with a veneer of despair. I thought that if I looked too closely into those lost years, I might split apart altogether.

No one can prepare you for how all the beautiful and wonderful things in life can lift and inspire you while at the same time send you into the pits of despair. It's a marvelous, wonderful, toxic, horrifying, and unending series of events that's like being on a roller coaster ride from hell. You climb to the top of the hill of success only to be driven down into madness by watching your elderly parents grow old and die. You survive that and climb up out of madness only to be driven back down into the pits watching your children struggle and your marriage fall apart.

And yet we become attached to our roller-coaster lives because the ride is all we know. I was so confined by my roles that I became numb and frozen inside on automatic pilot.

It's a kind of living death. Some people remain numb their entire lives, using it as a shield against loneliness, isolation, fear, anxiety, and depression. Some of us are thrown off the roller coaster when tragedy strikes, and we are hurled far away into a new reality where our old, safe roles no longer fit.

Suddenly I saw the ride for the illusion that it is. My old roles no longer fit, and I longed to shed them but didn't know how. It baffled me. What would I do? Who would I become? In other words, I was searching desperately to create new roles and a new life for myself. I thought I could do it the same way I did in the past, through force of will. I would simply focus on what I wanted and then figure out how to make it happen. But I didn't know what I wanted; I was always finding some new, intriguing possibility. I remember hearing about cranial sacral work and wondering whether I could do that. Or maybe I could try out living in an ashram or a spiritual community for a few months. The possibilities were overwhelming and for the first time in my life, I let go of asserting my will and just went along for the ride. I wouldn't say I trusted in the divine in the beginning—that took a while—rather, I just let go.

I heard that the psilocybin in hallucinogenic mushrooms could aid in the process of releasing old attachments and finding new meaning in life. I always said my mind was like a steel trap and I could control it. I never really believed that I could be affected by a hallucinogenic. I believed in my own egoic projection that I was mentally strong and in control. So when a mushroom journey came my way, I was nervous, but I didn't really believe much would happen beyond maybe relaxing and getting a good night's sleep.

My mushroom voyage involved partaking of a tea in a ceremonial setting with four friends who had done ceremonial mushrooms before. When offered the tea, I drank at least half and somehow spilled the rest. Someone said that was probably because I only needed that much. But after a half an hour of anticipation, nothing seemed to be happening. Then I drank more. Suddenly, what my rational mind believed to be a slight distortion of reality slowly began and then intensified. My friends' faces changed and morphed into beings and creatures, and I saw in the changes evidence of their past incarnations. One of my friends became an alien creature, red with long, hanging tentacles like an octopus. Another became a fairy creature with blue skin and shimmering wings, similar to the fairy creature I saw when I was a young girl. I saw in another all her past incarnations as priestesses.

Patterns and colors spun in my head—spirals of animals to the left and spirals of symbols on the right. The colors were vivid, all the colors of the rainbow spinning and taking me deeper and even down into the double helix of the spiral of life. It was magical and yet it was too much. I begged for it to stop so I could take a break, but there was no way out. The mushrooms were going to have their way with me. The intensity was devastatingly beautiful. I was at its mercy, begging to be out and yet wishing to stay forever.

My friends, four beautiful spiritual beings, were there to love and support me. It was magical and uncomfortable at the same time. For me, being on the giving end of beautiful, loving magic is much more comfortable than being the recipient. It was love in its purest form—nonsexual, nonjudgmental, and shamanic. Negative energy stored in my physical and energy bodies seemed to flow out of me. The music was magical—I could see music and follow it through the channels in my brain. Candles reacted to the energy in the room and danced to the music. Aliens came to visit and were part of us all and in us all.

I revisited death and my desire to die. I found myself back in the pain and railing at death for not having the courage to take me too. In that moment I felt that death was afraid of me. I saw and felt the presence of death as a guiding angel, a vast presence of serene calm, and I knew that it was not afraid of me and I was not afraid of it. I realized that death came to set Ben and me free from the chains of our old lives. Still I railed at death and said I would rather be constrained by my old life with Ben in it than have been set free. I didn't ask to be set free and I didn't ask for change. Death gently pointed out that nevertheless we both had been set free and given the opportunity to create something new. Ben had seized the opportunity and I knew he was content and growing into a new life on the other side. Now death asked me whether I had the courage to embrace change.

I saw myself as a light being, trying my best to rise but held down by shackles. As I heard myself telling death that yes, I had the courage, I saw the shackles fade away. Even the chains that bound me to my precious daughter were unbound, allowing me to forge a new relationship with her. Instead of a relationship based on fear and what I thought a mother should be, it could be a new relationship based only on love. I saw how I had tethered her to me and constrained her by the fearful mother role I played with the best intentions of keeping her safe. As I released that fearful mother role, I saw her begin to rise in her own beauty, connected to me only by love.

The mushroom journey dissipated after about four hours and bit by bit the spinning animals and symbols left my brain, my friends returned to their human forms, and music left my eyes and returned to my ears. The next day I was exhausted and exhilarated at the same time. I remembered vividly all that occurred, especially that I told death I had the courage to change.

I realized that holding on to the role of the grieving mother was keeping me stuck and frozen in despair. I learned during my shamanic training and in Gregg Braden's wonderful book *The Divine Matrix* that everything in the universe is made up of energy—vibrating masses of particles of quantum information that constantly change from waves to particles and back again. This means grief can change too, but only by observing and allowing other possibilities to come.

Slowly, one by one, I was able to let go of my other attachments—to my home, my job, and my possessions. These attachments were causing me great pain and yet I hadn't had the courage to take the first step. Then one day, as I sat in my office and thought about my vow to death to have the courage to change, I decided to take the first step. Instead of merely contemplating retirement, I called the personnel office and asked to have "my numbers run," what we called the process of contacting the personnel office to find out what one's retirement was worth. The day I found out my numbers would allow me to retire at the age of 62 was the day my life began to change. From that point on, it was as though the universe put a gale-force wind at my back, and in short order I retired, sold my home of 30 years and my possessions, and ended up embarking on the journey of a lifetime.

At the moment I decided to take action and look into retirement I had no idea what would be on the other end. I only knew that I needed and wanted to release the constraints of my old life and begin something fresh and new. I was asked many times what I was going to do after I retired. I could honestly reply that I had no idea, and for the first time in my life, I had no desire to fill in the details. Instead I allowed the endless possibilities opening up before me to pull me forward and have their way with me.

All I know for sure is when you are ready, you allow your life to change. You are no longer frozen in despair and hopelessness or locked down into the cycle of misery, fear, and avoidance. You see the way out of darkness into the light and you choose the light. Letting go of attachments for me was like cutting ropes to heavy boulders keeping me bound to my old ways.

THE BEAUTY WAY

How can the bird that is born for joy sit in a cage and sing?
— WILLIAM BLAKE

The beauty way is the practice of remembering to stop for a moment and find the beauty around us even when in our grieving we seem to be surrounded by hopelessness and despair.

After Ben's death, I remember feeling like nothing would ever be lovely or wonderful again. And I didn't want to even consider letting anything in. Until beauty landed on me— quite literally! Right after Ben died, I was at a Compassionate Friends meeting for those who lost a child. The meeting took place at a conservatory and there was a gathering on the lawn afterward to allow us to release a butterfly into the gardens. The butterfly is symbolic of transformation and rebirth and the journey of our loved ones. As we released the butterfly, we were to envision our loved one soaring freely.

I didn't like it and didn't want to participate, but my daughter had dragged me, so I went along with it. In my mind the entire exercise was hokey, and I refused to believe releasing a butterfly would somehow equate to seeing Ben soaring in eternal life. I was locked tightly into my grief and I wasn't about to let go. And yet my butterfly turned out to be the most amazing creature, even though I released it with determined ill humor. It flew away and then circled back to me and perched on my sweater directly over my heart, its head pointed toward my face, and it seemed to be contemplating me. People were pointing and smiling as I walked around with the butterfly attached to me. My daughter was smiling too, and after a while, I couldn't help but delight in it.

When it was time to leave and we were walking to the car, the butterfly was still with me. I wondered what I should do with it. Would it go home with me? As I walked, it traveled up my chest, over my throat, and stopped for a moment on my nose, looking me in the eyes before taking off and circling around my head all the way to the car. It hovered for a moment and then soared away, waving its wings. It was Ben, I knew, coming to cheer me up by bringing a bit of beauty to me.

You might wonder how I became such a sourpuss, refusing to see beauty until it landed on me. I believe it started in law school. I remember vividly the long hours reading, writing, and studying and the anxiety of trying to find my place in this new and alien world. I was one of the few to come to Georgetown University Law Center from a state school, the University of Pittsburgh. And I was one of the few who did not come from a family of wealth and privilege.

The very first day of school, the fact that my background was very different from other students hit me in the face. I was dressed in faded jeans, a plaid work shirt, and ratty sneakers. Other girls were dressed in skirts with twin-set sweaters and pearls. They had ways of dressing, styling their hair, and even being that were completely foreign to me. It really was a lot like the movie Legally Blonde, starring Reese Witherspoon. There were lots of wealthy, privileged kids who seemed to believe the world really was theirs for the taking, and then there were the rest of us.

In order to afford law school I had to work. I found a job at a consulting firm on the basis of my prior experience in hospital administration and master's degrees in public health and public and international affairs. I went to school during the day and worked at the firm every day from 4 P.M. to 10 P.M. Then I went home to study until the early hours of the next morning. I was exhausted all the time. When Christmas and spring break came, I took them as opportunities to work more hours at the consulting firm to have a little extra money. I looked longingly at the lifestyles of my classmates who spent their holidays at exotic locations lounging in the sun, all paid for by mom and dad. I was determined to do whatever it took to become one of them. So I worked as hard as I could and forgot about everything else.

During law school, one of the teaching assistants said to me, "Take time to smell the roses." It stopped me in my tracks, and I remember it to this day. I think it struck me so hard because it was completely inconsistent with the paradigm of success I was buying into. It did not fit with my conditioning of hard work and no play as the formula for success. From time to time that experience rose up to taunt me, but I pushed it away. Those roses were beautiful, but they had thorns. Just like in fairy tales, you could be pricked and life could change for the worse. I might lose my edge; I might not be successful. Better to avoid beauty altogether.

I worked hard then and for the next 30 years; I had bought into the concept of success at any price. My parents moved in with us to help take care of my children so I was able to work long hours without having to worry about picking them up from day care. I felt that evenings and weekends were enough time with my children. I felt proud of how few vacations I took, even family vacations. I believed that the time I spent getting ahead at work was justified by the kind of life I could afford for my children. Sometimes I even sent my husband off on vacations with my children without me so I could have a "staycation" and work, take care of my aging parents, and catch up on housework.

I spent my time and money taking care of my kids and parents and house in a very unconscious and programmed way because this is what my mother did, and probably her mother too. Cooking and cleaning were a never-ending exercise. I was taught that if you don't get up early and get to work, "you won't amount to a row of pins," and that "idle hands are the devil's workshop."

My work commute was treacherous; a traffic accident on one of the major arteries and an hour commute could easily become a blur of one and a half or two hours. Working and commuting and running errands on the weekends pretty much took up my time. Busy, busy, busy, and looking to stay busy on and on, forevermore, no matter what.

I wasn't happy. I mostly felt overwhelmed and frustrated, but I was unable to imagine a different way of being. The demands of daily life left no time for imagination. Besides, imagination could only lead to reflecting on where and how my life had gone so very wrong. Better to fill daytime to the brim and make sure there were enough sleeping pills beside the bed to avoid any unbearable 3 A.M. reflections.

I was not alone in my madness. It is a collective madness of those of us who live in the D.C. metropolitan area. We are blind to beauty, and the story of Joshua Bell illustrates this perfectly. Joshua Bell is a world-famous violinist who, in 2007, disguised himself and played six classical pieces for 43 minutes during rush hour at Washington D.C.'s L'Enfant Plaza Metro station. He played a violin worth $3.5 million, and he played one of the most intricate pieces ever written. Approximately 1,100 people passed through the station, most of them rushing to work. In those 43 minutes, only 7 people stopped and stayed awhile, and 27 gave him money but continued to walk on. He collected $32, and when he stopped playing no one applauded or noticed.

This was organized by *The Washington Post* as an experiment in perceiving beauty in a commonplace environment at an inappropriate hour. The experiment showed how programmed we are to avoid beauty and stay on course. It wasn't as if Joshua Bell's playing was at fault. Three days earlier, at a socially acceptable time and place, he played to a sold-out concert in Boston, where good tickets cost $100. It was all of us worker bees who could not be coaxed out of our collective madness.

I was a slave to the fears, desires, and expectations of success at any price for 30 years. I would have been one of those who walked by Joshua Bell. I might have had a moment of longing for the freedom to stop and listen, but the constraints of duty and habit would have overridden such foolishness. I was so strongly in the grip of the life I created that neither a week of vacation nor tarrying a moment to delight in music could call me away. The tight grip of routine had taken over my very life force and squashed even the desire for change.

Is success at any price all about greed? I found an answer in the works of Alain de Botton, a philosopher and author who makes philosophy practical and accessible. He argues that it's not that we are particularly materialistic, but rather that we live in a society that extends emotional rewards to the acquisition of material goods, and we crave the rewards. Social acceptance, admiration, pride, and often, even love. These are not to be sneezed at! I gave a lot to attain these rewards.

And then Ben died. The too-familiar house and job and routines I put in place to provide constancy and support for Ben and my daughter and myself became confining rather than rewarding. Death challenged my slumbering soul to wake and open my eyes. As I looked through the eyes of bereavement and the mental storm death created inside me, those familiar structures were revealed as carefully crafted prison walls. My daughter had grown and had her own life. Ben had transitioned and had his own life. And as for me, I had a choice—life within my familiar prison walls or walk with great intent and purpose to the doorway, putting the key to my confinement into the lock, twisting, and walking free.

Freedom entailed changing my perspective on how I looked at everyday matters by actively making an effort to find beauty around me. I had to let go of the sourpuss viewpoint that I was so accustomed to and that, in my grief, I had perfected and enshrouded myself. I knew Ben didn't want me to live a guilt-ridden life. Yet I felt guilty about even thinking of enjoying life or making time to allow beauty in my life. How could I do that? My son was dead, and beauty was inconsistent with mourning, it seemed to me.

And yet after my experience with the butterfly and the delight I felt, I knew Ben had stepped in to show me this practice was important. He wanted me to focus on finding beauty and make it part of mourning. I remember running out of laundry detergent and feeling extremely frustrated at myself for not remembering to pick up some. Frustrated me was ready to make an angry and self-denigrating trip to the store. Suddenly, I stood still and thought, *How can I turn this around? How can I see the beauty in this predicament?* And then it came to me. *What if I just played hooky from laundry and went out on my lovely tree house–like back porch, sat for a while, and maybe read a book?* It felt wonderful.

I had to make this an everyday practice because guilt and mourning were so overwhelming that it seemed easier to give it up. I had to remind myself to find beauty in some way every day, so I wrote the word *beauty* on a note card and stuck it on my refrigerator door. At some point during the day, the note would catch my attention and I would force myself to make the effort to find something I could do that would bring beauty into my life.

I was always fascinated by sunsets but rarely made time for them. In fact I didn't actually remember making time to see a single one in the 25 years I lived in my house. I looked up the sunset time and I made a date with myself to find somewhere from which to watch it. Since I hadn't paid attention to sunsets for years, it took a bit of driving around to find a good spot. It was fun at first, but then old thoughts crept in, like *I don't have time to do this every day.* And I found myself laughing at myself and saying, "Oh, really?"

There were also cloudy-day excuses that popped up and I had to resist saying, "Oh well, [sigh of relief] no beauty today!" I learned to find beauty sitting and watching the rain come in. To see the dark clouds on the horizon and feel the wind beginning to move and turn the leaves on the maple trees upside down. To watch as slow, gentle rain fell or massive storm clouds spitting lightning billowed toward me. I found nearby temples and churches to explore that I never noticed in 25 years. I made phone calls to friends whom I hadn't spoken to for years. I bought flowers for myself and took flowers to friends for no reason. Instead of saying no to invitations, I started saying yes.

It was a process of breaking the habit of allowing days, weeks, and months to pass by numbly. Slowly, a new habit formed that replaced the old habit. The new habit was one of seeing beauty and life all around me every day, feeling it and living it. In this process I developed a new relationship with Ben. He no longer appeared frantic or guilty to me. It never occurred to me that the extent of my grief also affected him in a negative way. I sensed his presence most when I was somewhere happily pursuing a new and beautiful experience.

All I know for sure is that allowing the pursuit of beauty back into my life helped to lift the great burden of despair and hopelessness that I carried for so long. I was still sad, I missed Ben's physical presence greatly, but I found myself lighter of spirit as time passed.

Exercises to Apply the Practices of the South Direction of the Medicine Wheel and Begin the Process of Transforming Our Lives

Start by finding a notebook, a pen or pencil, a candle, and a small tin pie pan or tray. The pan will be used to catch ashes later in the exercise. In this exercise, you will write honest answers to four questions, then set an intent, hold them to the candle flame, and burn them. By burning them you release them to your concept of God, or Spirit, or Universe for your healing. Then allow your heart to open to allow in new ways of filling the newly freed space.

If you would rather light a fire in your fireplace or outside, that's fine too. In shamanic mythology, fire is a path of rapid transformation, so by burning your answers you allow rapid transformation into your life. There's no need to worry that someone might find your answers because you will be burning them. This will allow you to be completely and radically honest in your answers because no one will see them but you.

Next find somewhere you can sit alone in stillness with your notebook, pen or pencil, candle, and pie pan beside you. Allow yourself this alone time when you have nowhere to go and nothing to do. As you sit, concentrate on your in-breath and your out-breath. When we breathe, we empty our lungs of old, stale air so fresh, new air can come in. Our breath is a metaphor for the exercises in this book. We are in the process of breathing out old, stale ways of being so new ones have space to live inside us. In solitude we can hear the voices inside ourselves that grow faint and are drowned out by the noise and busyness of our daily lives and by the presence of other people. Stay still until you are in a place of knowing that what you are hearing is the subtle voice of your spirit. Stay until the doors and walls you have erected around your broken heart are open. Once you feel ready, ask yourself the questions below and answer with radical honesty. That means no holds barred, nothing held back, courageously naming that which must be named for your transformation.

Ask yourself each of the following questions one at a time and immediately take your answer to the fire before moving on to the next question.

Ask yourself who you are judging and who you think is judging you before or after your loved one died. Who wounded you deeply? Who wounded your loved one? Who disappointed you? Who disappointed your loved one? Make a list. The list might include you or your loved one. It could include hospitals or doctors. It might include your sister or brother, father or mother, or grandparents. Then focus on each one and turn each one into a tree. See how they have twisted themselves to survive and to try to find the light. See each one reaching for the light.

When you have finished, burn your list in your candle flame or fire with the intention of letting go of all the judgment, and allow the smoke of the fire to carry it all to the light. As judgment is released, imagine your heart opening to allow in peace and clarity.

Ask yourself how your suffering is connected to shame, blame, and guilt over things that happened in the past. Make a list of each action or word or circumstance that causes you to feel shame, blame, or guilt. Ask yourself whether it is true that you had control. Is it true that you caused your loved one's pain? Is it true that you could have made your loved one choose differently? Is it true that your suffering demonstrates the depth of your love? Do the same thing with anyone else you are blaming—hospitals, doctors, friends, or relatives, or even God. When you have finished, burn your list in your candle flame or fire with the intent to release the stories and feed your suffering to the fire. Envision the smoke transforming and releasing your suffering. Allow your heart to open and allow in the clarity and peace of loving memory.

Ask yourself how the structures of the life you created Before Death Day have become confining. Make a list of all the things that you are attached to. What and who are you afraid to let go of? What would happen if you let go and walked away? When you have finished, burn your list in your candle flame or fire and envision the flames releasing your attachments and your heart opening to the light of transformation.

Ask yourself where you find beauty in life. If you have trouble with this, go back in time and remember what used to bring you in touch with beauty. List them all. Then ask yourself what is keeping you from those places. List those too. When you have finished, burn your list in your candle flame or fire with the intention of releasing anything keeping you from experiencing beauty and opening your heart to allow beauty to grow inside you and transform your life.

CHAPTER THREE

West Practices of the Medicine Wheel

Becoming Lighter

*Unexpressed emotions will never die. They are buried alive
and they will come forth later in uglier ways.*

— SIGMUND FREUD

*A wise woman once said, "Fuck this shit,"
and she lived happily ever after.*

— UNKNOWN

The West direction is about dying. Familiar territory, you
say? Not exactly. In the mythology of the Four Winds medicine wheel, the West is the direction of the jaguar, the spiritual
warrior. As we did to old emotional patterns and ancestral and
cultural conditioning, we let go of limiting beliefs about self-
worth, abundance, and intimate relationships with ourselves
and others. We let go of the beliefs that family, society, culture,

genetics, and karma delivered to our doorway by the river of life as we came into this world and every day since. As we bring these beliefs and conditioning from the abstract into our focus and awareness, insights begin to unfold that help to bring old stories to light. Releasing these stories continues the process we began in the South direction of gaining access to what is real, the pain of our loss.

These are the practices of the West: not colluding with the consensual, nondoing, certainty, and fearlessness. I was pretty sure once I read just the names of these practices that I had been doing everything wrong. I might have been a poster child for embodying the consensual. I had never considered nondoing to be even one of my minor virtues. I felt wracked by uncertainty and lost in fear. Would I be able to understand these practices, and could they help me on my journey through grief? Could I thwart the irresistible undertow pulling me back toward center stream to float in the stagnant currents of all that I had absorbed from my culture, my ancestors, and my upbringing? Or could I choose to look boldly and allow the insights and wisdom to light the way forward out of darkness and despair? Would I have the courage to crawl out onto the beach, naked and washed clean from the past?

Just as you did with the practices of the South direction, jot down anything that you find relevant to your own life as you read my story. The exercises at the end of this chapter will help you work with these practices and continue your journey through the transformation process.

NOT COLLUDING WITH THE CONSENSUAL

While climbing the ladder of success, make sure the ladder is leaning against the right building.
— STEPHEN COVEY

This one always seemed big to me, and important. Even the words sound very important. Imagine waking up and saying to yourself, "Today I am not going to collude with the consensual!" Wow, and how do I do that exactly? If the consensual is all the things that we in our culture agree upon, then those are a lot of things. For example: it's important to be successful; it's so important to be at work on time, we dare not tarry for a few minutes to listen to a renowned musician playing in a subway station on our way to work; and making sure our kids are scheduled to the max to ensure that they, too, experience success. And maybe it's hard to grasp all the ways we have bought into consensual thinking because some of the things are rolling around our unconscious mind and subtly affect where we choose to live and who we choose as friends.

And the word *collude* is also a heavy one. By definition it includes the concept of willfully cooperating secretly or unlawfully to deceive. It seems to be such a heavy concept. Did I willfully cooperate? I did by buying into success at any price. Did I do it secretly? I suppose I did. I certainly didn't rail against it. I just went along day by day making choices that acquiesced to the expectations floating around me. Who did I deceive? Probably myself most of all, every day, as I made choices that kept me locked in and blindly running on the hamster wheel I created.

Looking back on my life, I realized that I not only had little interest in living when Ben passed but also long before. I think I was, as the phrase goes, "bored to death" or "bored senseless," but I marched along one foot firmly planted in front of the other, fearing to step away. But when life as I knew it ended abruptly, I was left with two choices: rise up out the ashes of my old life or live a life of misery and pain in the ashes of the old one. One result of being bored to death or bored senseless was the mindless accumulation of a houseful of stuff that was now weighing me down. Comedian George Carlin did a great stand-up routine about "stuff" that stuck with me. You do know that you don't own your stuff, right? It owns you!

I spent a lifetime accumulating my stuff and taking care of my house, my parents, and my kids. I really couldn't imagine life after retirement or what I would do with myself. Maybe I would keep working until I turned 80, or maybe even 90, when illness would take me out. I pretty much had it made with respect to job security. I had a lifetime appointment, and there was precedent for judges to work late in life: the chief judge was 87 and still working, and another judge worked into his 90s.

In retrospect, it seems clear to me that I busily acquired stuff because I was addicted to the high of retail therapy. I lost myself in malls or spent hours shopping online. Then there was the added delicious benefit of having all those wonderful purchases delivered to my front door the very next day! Most of my stuff wasn't really important or necessary, but having a lot of stuff was very important to my ego. Ultimately, even though I spent a boatload of money on myself, my house, and my kids, I still felt frustrated and empty. All the stuff didn't make my kids any happier and my house was a bottomless money pit of keeping up with the neighbors.

I sometimes wondered why acquiring stuff didn't make me happy. Looking back on it, I think it was because the underlying motivation was my discomfort with and alienation from my own feelings, fears, and frustrations. I lost the ability to really connect with life, so why not isolate myself and pack down my frustrations and fears with another round of buying more stuff? I knew most of what I was acquiring was meaningless—that's why I ended up referring to it as *stuff*, the plural, generalized term used to describe the myriad of objects we acquire that end up lost in the back of a closet or in the garage or a storage bin.

My stuff temporarily soothed my ego because the excitement of the chase and acquisition temporarily shielded me from uncomfortable emotions. However, in a day or so, I found even the most expensive and exciting purchases ended up in the place of my psyche where I stored my "already acquired stuff," and I was on the prowl once again for the next big-ticket item to keep my emotions at bay. After Ben died, retail therapy no longer appealed to me. I found myself having to figure out what to do next, bereft of comfort. Cold turkey.

My judicial position put me in daily contact with colleagues whose values I no longer shared at a job that I believed had no meaning other than preserving the bottom line of the privileged owners and investors in corporations I found to be manipulative and without conscience. It was common to hear another judge say they wanted to "die with" their "boots on," a euphemism for staying on the job until they died. I never really aspired to that philosophy, but I certainly remember thinking I had no idea what I would do when I retired, as I really had no interests outside of work and taking care of my house and Ben. Or at least not enough interests to fill my days after retirement.

What in the world would I do to fill all that empty time? I observed colleagues of mine retiring only to ask to return to work after a few months. They complained that life was empty and they had nothing to do. I certainly equated retirement as the occasional annual vacation interspersed with movies and dining out preceded and followed by a whole lot of empty lonely days. One thing about commuting in the second-worst traffic in the country to and from 8- to 10-hour workdays was that the daily grind masked a lot of unhappiness. Once that was gone, one had a lot of time to fill.

Many people consent to the herd mentality and keep each other going by bragging about how long they work and trading stories about how they manage to beat the traffic or survive the long metro commute. At their very essence, these behaviors are designed to keep us in line with consensual reality as determined by the herd.

The herd mentality tells us we need to stay together to be safe. If you go off by yourself, you could get lost. In the herd, one of the most powerful punishments is shunning—because then you don't have the protection of the group and you are alone and vulnerable. Shunning is practiced by religious groups, families, and professional groups to control their members. Just ask a professional of any persuasion to act outside the rules of that profession. They will tell you that they will be mocked at best and kicked out of the profession at worst.

When did I agree to this behavior? When I was younger, I used to refer to "them," the ones in power, the ones calling the shots. Then I realized that there is no "them," only "us." We all conspire and collude in creating the herd mentality and raising our young to run on the hamster wheel of consensual reality. After all, the wheel provides us with nice stuff and security. A place to live and good food to eat and fun things to do—at appropriate times. Life off the wheel may look pretty, but that's where hunger and poverty and homelessness lie.

Fear-based decision-making about life is what kept me in the same place, doing the same things day after day. I heard that most of us live our lives in the same five-mile radius day after day, week after week. The familiar dry cleaner, the familiar grocery store, the familiar restaurants. Even the idea of going to a different grocery store felt overwhelming. Why should I even try? I knew where everything was in the familiar one and I could rush home and rush through there and then rush to make dinner in an unconscious way so I could turn on the TV and remain unconscious until bedtime. Maybe I would be lucky enough to fall asleep with three or four Tylenol PM. Maybe not.

When my children were young, I felt proud that I compensated for my busy life and neglected children by coming home and immediately jumping into my car and driving my overly scheduled children to a myriad of activities. Nothing is more unsettling than to talk to other parents who have their children in more activities than yours because that means their children might have a leg up in the competitive market in which they must learn to live. We are under extreme pressure to teach our precious children the ways of the hamster wheel. To value it and it alone. To stay on it and not be seduced by the beauty of the world outside. And when one of them strays or is not as successful as their peers, we are apologetic and make excuses for them. We are embarrassed. We have failed.

In *Awakening from the Daydream*, David Nichtern writes about aspects of the Wheel of Life as depicted in Buddhist allegorical painting. He discusses six realms that we co-create on the basis of past and present thoughts, actions, and karma, and in which we are lost in the daydream of our creation. I found his depiction of the Jealous God Realm to fit the world that I found myself in. The Jealous God Realm is "dominated by jealousy and competition," and even though its inhabitants "may have position and respect . . . their perch is too precarious to be stable, and they expend a lot of energy to establish and maintain it." The main obstacle to finding peace in this realm is "living in a world of paranoia, jealousy, relentless competition, and one-upmanship."

According to Alain de Botton in his book *Status Anxiety*, it's not that we should give up on success, but we should make sure it is our own, what we really want, so we are truly the authors of our own ambitions. Otherwise we are at risk of finding out, at the end of our success journey, that it wasn't what we wanted all along. I completely agree because that is what happened to me. It took my son's death to shake me awake and see how miserable my life had become.

Death came to my door and my emotions were raw and exposed and very much awake. No coping skill worked any longer. I couldn't shop my way out of it because stuff no longer mattered. I couldn't jump back on the hamster wheel because being part of the consensual reality around me no longer mattered either. I had been thrown off the wheel and I lay dazed and bleeding in the new After Death Day territory.

All I know for sure is that I had to choose. I could try to live an empty, emotionless echo of my past life, neither here nor there, just going through the motions of the past. Or I could choose to walk away and reboot and reset. I saw an opportunity to transform the life I lived that was based on what was acceptable and conforming and lifeless into something with meaning and purpose. Something based on new dreams and aspirations that were truly mine.

NONDOING

Search your heart and see
the way to do is to be.

— Lao Tsu

Nondoing means letting go of micromanaging our lives and "making things happen." Instead it's a practice of allowing things to happen. It's letting go of the illusion that we are in control and must remain hypervigilant or something terrible will happen. It's letting go of keeping busy as a way to avoid uncomfortable emotions and letting yourself just be present and available for long, deep conversations with others and maybe even with yourself.

Being available to having deep conversations with ourselves puts us in touch with the Observer Within. What is the Observer Within? I now know that it is that part of us that we have forgotten and was hidden by our busy lives. It is that part of us that has never been born and has never died; it is our enlightened nature that does not want us to suffer. Once we are in touch with our Observer, our soul, our Buddhahood, our enlightened selves, we see through all of our busyness to all those painful things we tried to avoid.

No matter how hard I tried and how diligent and frenzied I became, something inevitably fell through the cracks anyway. I was not the only person I knew who avoided stillness. I have a friend who ingeniously divided the weekend into seven parts—one on Friday night; then Saturday morning, afternoon, and evening; and Sunday morning, afternoon, and evening. Each part had to be scheduled and filled or disaster might strike. She might have to contemplate the reality she created and find pain and suffering. Being busy doesn't fool the Observer Within, who so clearly sees what we have created for ourselves.

But my overscheduled life gave me the illusion of safety. If I stayed busy, I never had to look at how I really felt about my spouse, my children, my job, or my life. I believed that I had created everything around me by force of will, that there was no other way to get through life successfully, and success was important. I avoided looking too closely at what I had created. I had to believe that my marriage was good, my job was great, and my children well taken care of. I had to believe that I could handle it all, that I was Superwoman!

Otherwise I might have to confront deep sadness and fear and loneliness.

Thirteen years before Ben died, I spent a year outside of the Washington D.C. area working at an agency about five hours from home. It was the first job offered to me and, as usual, I grabbed the brass ring of success. It was difficult to leave my beloved children, who were only in the sixth and seventh grades, each week. I was only able to come home on the weekends. I was married and we ended up buying a lake house near my new job so they could all come to visit. I wasn't familiar with any meditation traditions at that point, but in the evenings when I was alone at the lake house, my mind would begin to relax deeply while I was looking at the beauty of the lake. Even though I felt guilty for not being at home, for the first time in a long time my evenings were free to do nothing but sit and reflect. I had time to just be. Reflection gave me insight into my unhappy marriage.

I acknowledged to myself that my marriage was causing much stress and anxiety. I also acknowledged how difficult life was with the demands of teenage children and elderly parents all living under one roof. Away in my lake house, I didn't have to worry about the details of everyday living, like cleaning and cooking or monitoring homework. Although I worked 40 to 50 hours a week, my evenings were free, and for once I didn't fill the time with projects. Although the obsessively neat and project-oriented part of me anxiously noted that the walls needed painting and the carpets needed steam cleaning, I simply didn't do it.

It occurred to me that I felt completely invisible at my family home. I decided to test out my theory when I was there one weekend. I wondered if my spouse would notice if I remained completely silent at a dinner out. He didn't. I wondered, too, about my parents and children. What would happen if I went about doing all the things I normally did around the house, like cleaning and cooking, but silently? No one noticed. How about if I dyed my blonde hair red? It took three weeks for my spouse to notice. I really was the invisible woman, completely alone and lonely and unnoticed. I really didn't know what to do or how to fix it.

As I continued my nightly vigils at the lake, I had a flash of insight that my constant busy juggling of so many balls was putting a barrier between me and my family. But I couldn't see how to take away any of the balls. I could only see getting through the next week or the next month and hoping that a miracle would occur. I felt that something terrible would happen if I lost control and the balls began to fall to the floor.

What if I faced the fact that I was alone and lonely in my marriage? What would happen then? A divorce would split our little family apart emotionally and financially. I wasn't sure I could raise two kids on my own. I hoped to maybe keep everything together by just putting one foot continually ahead of the other and refusing to look at any other options. Better to be invisible than alone and afraid.

Eventually I began to consider making changes to my life, and the first change was a divorce. I saw change as a glide path, not a critical event, so changes had to be made gradually. I had children, and my parents lived with us, so I didn't want to come in one day and upset the applecart of our lives. It was the classic scenario with dependent young children and elderly parents all needing my time and attention. Anyone who has been there knows it's difficult and demanding and leaves little energy for anything else. But isn't that exactly the point—by creating busy lives that encourage no time for thought or stillness, we make sure that those lives remain locked in so we feel safe from the scariness of change. It took several years, but eventually the divorce was final. That was one less ball to juggle.

The divorce helped to alleviate some of the stress. Then my parents died, and my daughter went off to college. I was no longer sandwiched in, taking care of two generations. At that point, it was just Ben and me left in a household that used to have six people, three generations, and five dogs, who also began to die one by one. I had less to do than I ever had before, but my concern for Ben more than made up for it. Before Ben's death, I hung on desperately to hope and continued my busy dance that kept fear at bay. Really, I was just keeping my head down in the sand like an ostrich while in the meantime my ass was exposed and waving in the air. If our heads are safe, then so are we—right? Nope.

Ben's sudden and unexpected death changed everything. There was no longer a need to be busy, there was nothing more to fear; he was gone. At first it was terrifying to have so many empty hours of unfilled time stretching ahead of me. I often found myself thinking of things I could do to fill those hours. For the first few months after Ben's death, time just seemed to float by me. Hours went by as I sat or lay on his bed and did nothing.

I used to wish for time to do nothing but managed to fill that time with "just needing to" do this or that for a few minutes that could turn into hours. Well, too bad that time for nondoing didn't work out today, I would think. Maybe tomorrow. It became a game that I played with myself, scheduling time and then undermining it, scheduling and undermining, scheduling and undermining. Since what I was really doing was avoiding uncomfortable thoughts and emotions, undermining won.

But after Ben died, I got the hang of letting go. It was . . . relaxing. My body began to tune in to my muscles and tendons in an unfamiliar way. I noticed the difference between having everything tensed up like I was ready to flee or ward off an attack and being relaxed. My mind stopped obsessively setting goals and activities. Now I had no to-do list, no one to clean or shop for, no elderly parents to make appointments for, and few responsibilities. The balls I had worked so hard to keep in the air had all dropped. In time I became familiar with my Observer Within and began to sit with all the emotions I avoided for so long.

All I know for sure is that all the emotions I tried to avoid by keeping my head in the sand or being busy were waiting for me. Sitting with each one of them—sadness, fear, remorse, regret, despair, anger, disgust, hopelessness, guilt—brought me home to my true self. The one who was no longer in the grip of conforming to what others wanted. The one who was free to live life on her own terms. The one who could even be courageous enough to transform her life.

CERTAINTY

If you walk, just walk. If you sit, just sit;
but whatever you do, don't wobble.

— ZEN MASTER UMMON

The practice of certainty involves cultivating the ability to commit fully to a course of action. We don't allow ourselves to be derailed by excuses like not being good enough, thin enough, pretty enough, smart enough, well enough, rich enough, young enough, old enough, et cetera. We simply get on with it, even shutting the escape hatches. Instead of saying, "If this doesn't work out, I can just go back to whatever it was I was doing before," we choose to blow up the bridge behind us, leaving no alternative to marching forward.

Conceptually, certainty seemed like a great way to move forward, kind of like a military campaign. But my life had never been based on certainty; rather, it seemed like I mostly bobbled along trying to avoid what I didn't want and grabbed on to whatever came my way that looked pretty good. Maybe looking at my past and my choices would help me discover some essential part of myself.

I remember my teacher going around my seventh-grade classroom and asking each of us what we wanted to be when we grew up. Usually, it was doctors for the boys and nurses for the girls. Groupthink was powerful that day—not even a fireman or policeman was thrown in the mix. We knew the drill: go with the flow and don't stand out. But when it got to me, I had a momentary surge of independence and I called out, "Archaeologist!" Everyone sniggered and rolled their eyes, but that was usual for me. I was too tall, towering over the boys and the girls, I had braces, and I was smart and often in a dreamy daze from nonstop reading.

My mother took me to the local library every week and I would pick out seven books, one for each day. I tuned out the small-town world around me. Books were my salvation. They introduced me to different places and ways of being; they made me long to leave home as soon as possible, go to college, and do exciting things in a world far away. My parents and I did not travel. We didn't get in our car and take cross-country trips, nor did we travel internationally, not even to Canada or Mexico. We stayed close to home except for a one-week vacation to a nearby lake every year. This annual break was heaven to me and probably why I have chosen to live near lakes several times in my life.

College came around and I still wanted to become an archaeologist. I wanted out of the small town I grew up in and away from the small-time thinking. I didn't want to get married, have kids, or end up on the back of a motorcycle with one of the local Hells Angels. These plans were met with complete resistance by my parents and accusations that

I was trying to get out of their control and just wanted to shack up with some guy. This was pretty much the truth—I was not of my mother's generation, not even close. She was born in 1915 and I was born in 1953. She grew up in a large family during the Depression and I grew up as an only child during a time of relative financial ease. She grew up with and embraced the small-town morals endemic in that time, while I grew up watching the Beatles on TV and wanting desperately to be part of the culture of the '60s.

I was seven years younger than a cousin who attended the University of Michigan and was then thrown out in 1968 because he was the head of the Students for a Democratic Society and had engineered a sit-in as well as other activism connected to the Weathermen group, who were sought by the FBI. After being expelled he flew to India to study Transcendental Meditation with the Maharishi Mahesh Yogi. All of this was discussed in hush-hush tones as if it was something shameful. But to my 16-year-old mind it was magic. I pictured myself being part of a sit-in and hauled away by the police and longed for that to happen to me too.

I had never heard even the words *yogi* or *Transcendental Meditation* before, so I ran off to the library to find out more. The most exciting day of my young life was when my cousin came to visit and taught me a bit about meditation behind my parents' backs. He gave me the mantra—aim. I treasured this secret mantra. I was even more different from this small town now; I had a powerful secret, a mantra that I nurtured.

My father was a functioning alcoholic who was mostly off in his own world working long hours, playing golf, and drinking with his friends. While he loved me, he wasn't around much. He was fired from Westinghouse as part of a sweep of employees who were getting to be retirement eligible. It was doubtful whether there would be college money for me, and if there was, I wouldn't be going somewhere exciting like the University of Michigan. I would be living at home and attending a local branch of the University of Pittsburgh—not even getting as far away as the 20 miles to attend the main campus. I wanted to fly but my wings were always clipped. I totally related to the lines from William Blake's "The Schoolboy": "How can the bird that is born for joy, sit in a cage and sing?" I wanted to fly high and sing; I wanted adventures and freedom.

I found both in the form of a young teacher at my high school. I was beautiful, and smart, and I caught his eye. He was 24 to my 17, and the idea of an illicit romance under the nose of the school administration, my parents, and other students excited my rebel heart. We decided to get married. It was a big deal. My parents were furious. In their mind, if you had sex, you had to get married. To me this was an exciting step away from their control. My new husband supported me going to college. It was going to happen! Yes, it would be at the local branch of the University of Pittsburgh, but that campus was only for two years. After that I would be on my way to the main campus. At that moment I wasn't worried about how a marriage might hinder me. At that moment I was tasting freedom.

I went to college and studied anthropology and urban affairs and minored in French. I aced those two years at the local campus with a 4.0 average. I exceeded my expectations, and I outgrew my marriage and divorced in time for my third year at the main campus. In the mores of my small town, a 19-year-old divorcée was a scandal. I was the talk of the town and a disgrace to my family. I didn't care. I was another step to somewhere far away.

I excelled in the remainder of my undergraduate years, graduating a semester early, and went on to earn two master's degrees. My school had a Fulbright competition for students to go to Afghanistan. One hundred and four students competed for five spots. We were tested for language under-standing and cultural knowledge. I won one of the spots.

My parents were frantic with worry. This was 1974, long before the Internet and cell phones. International calls were difficult to make and involved the assistance of an inter-national operator. Communication was pretty much done through aerograms—blue paper on which you wrote on both sides and sometimes crosswise to get more in—and you could mail them cheaply. My parents didn't want me to go, but I insisted.

I'm not sure whether their greater concern was that I would be in another country or that I would bring a man home. In those days dating foreigners was frowned upon, at least in my hometown. And bringing home a man of color or of a different ethnicity was a definite no-no. I was enchanted by all these possibilities.

The program was jointly sponsored by the State Depart-ment and the Fulbright office. Before the Soviet Invasion, the U.S. kept influence and interests in the country through the exchange program. In those days Afghanistan really was the end of the earth to most of the students and their parents. Those were magical months of travel and explora-tion, and I returned home wanting more. But my parents, who had never traveled out of the country, were anxious to make sure I didn't do anything remotely like that again. They reminded me that I needed to do something practical to make a living and that living abroad was dangerous.

After I finished my master's degrees, I accepted an administrative position in a local hospital. I soon tired of the position, which largely involved trying to get money from indigent patients, Medicare, and Medicaid, and dealing with doctors who refused to wash their hands between patients. I applied and was accepted to Georgetown University Law Center and I was more than ready to go.

I graduated from Georgetown and clerked for traditional law firms. But the call of the wild was ever in my ear, and to the disapproval of my parents and the partners at my law firm, I left a promising job to become a Judge Advocate General's Corps (JAG Corps) officer in the U.S. Army. I was off to Korea and more adventure. I was a disappointment to my family and an oddball in my profession. I was counseled by the partners in my firm that I was ruining my life, that my law career would be over, and that I would never be a success.

I loved the Army and the adventure, and I married an Army officer. In short order we had two children. My husband was in the Special Forces but, as a result of an accident, was medically discharged. I followed him out of the military, found a civilian legal position, and began the process of climbing the ladder and grabbing any brass ring that came my way.

I don't exactly know how it happened, but at this point in my life, I lost my way. Working, marriage, raising children, taking care of aging parents, and taking care of a household defeated my adventurous spirit. I became so weighed down with duty and responsibility that I forgot how to have fun. All the pressures put me in survival mode. Because my husband had had several failed hip-replacement surgeries and several revisions, I never felt I could take a few years off and stay home. If the worst happened and a revision failed, it was possible he would have the hardware removed to allow the bone to heal. We were told he'd then be unable to walk at all for months or years. In my mind, I became the responsible one financially. The worst never happened, but it loomed over my head the entire time my children were growing up.

My husband and I were never equal partners after that. He had a devil-may-care attitude toward life and I was the diligent one. Opposites do attract, but sometimes only for a while. I carried the load, taking care of the house, the finances, and my parents. He was more likely to go off with the kids on an adventure so I could catch up at home. I so regret not taking more family vacations and spending more time with my kids rather than worrying too much about cleaning and laundry and work. Those many lost years, more than 30, were gone in the mists of time. I was so busy, I hardly remember the details. It's not that I was never present or never available, but mostly I was overwhelmed.

But here I was 30 years later, on the verge of starting over at age 62. Not because I wanted to but because the death of my son changed everything. There was no turning back or trying to fit into my old life. I now saw through eyes changed by grief. I had to ask myself the hard questions: What would I do if I could live my life any way I wanted? Could I imagine a life off the hamster wheel of job, house, stuff, and familiarity? Did I have the courage to transcend hopelessness and despair and search for meaning beyond what is traditional and expected?

After all I had spent more than 30 years as a lawyer. I knew I was bored to death with what I was doing, but what else was I good at? I was still learning how to be a shamanic healing practitioner and I really wasn't sure how I would make that work. Would I stay in my same house, keeping Ben's room as a shrine? Would I continue with the same five-mile radius of familiar shops and the terrible commute?

Those options felt tight and constraining and intensified my feelings of hopelessness and despair. I wanted more, but what? I thought to myself, *Look at your past. What were you doing before you lost your way? What would that rebellious, creative younger self do if she were standing here?* I decided to sit quietly and think of her and call her forgotten essence here to me now. I talked to her and cried and explained all that happened when I lost her and lost my way. I sobbed as I told her about Ben and about wanting desperately to figure out where to go from here. Where would I go? Who would I be? The answer that came to me was clear and simple. I would be far away—traveling and living a full and interesting life pursuing meaning and a spiritual path.

I felt that I had reconnected with a part of me that I had locked away. As I freed her, she took root in my heart. Her clear and simple guidance felt right, but it also seemed vague and lacking detail. But that was the way I operated in my rebellious, nonconforming past: I held the concept of what I wanted in my mind and opportunities arose that were consistent with my longings. Simple. I didn't worry about the details; I simply focused on finding opportunities. I knew this was a pivotal point. I either trusted this inner part of me that was vibrant and strong and newly freed, or I put her back in her cage and to her sadly constrained life. The soul doesn't have a lot of tolerance for doubt and fear. Do or don't, and be damned.

I was reenergized and revitalized—I was going to make it happen. I would go somewhere far away, I would travel a spiritual path and find meaning, and my life would be full and interesting. This became my daily mantra and it made me deliriously happy. So I retired. And once I did, things happened quickly. I took two weeks of vacation time to finish the Four Winds training. I then went on a vision quest with the Lakota and burned my judicial robes as a ceremonial giving to the fire, symbolically closing doors and burning my bridges behind me. There would be no going back to my old ways. I was on a journey to the future.

After the vision quest, I returned home, contacted a realtor, and immediately put my house on the market. It sold in three days, and I was out five weeks later, after hiring an auction house to empty my house of a lifetime of stuff. Friends and colleagues thought I was crazy to retire from an important high-status job and even more crazy to sell my house and my stuff to be homeless, traveling the world, and living in rental properties. And maybe I was. A friend even went to my daughter to persuade her to get me to change my mind because she felt I was still grieving and would later regret these decisions. My daughter told her, "I think my mom should shake her rattle and release her inner butterfly." How about that for unconditional love?

Here I was, two and a half years after Ben's death, finding the courage to make monumental life changes. Although some people thought I was crazy, I was surprised to find how many people were sympathetic and supportive. I was still crushed by my son's death and sobbed in supermarkets when people asked how I was. Finding the courage to make these life changes also made me brave enough to share feelings of failure and bereavement and hopelessness and wanting to die. To my surprise, friends, neighbors, and acquaintances began to open up about what was really going on in their lives. They, too, had kids they worried about and jobs they no longer related to. They, too, suffered death, divorce, and heartache and felt disconnected from life. We wept together and shared our heartbreaks and agreed that it was a relief to be able to stop pretending that everything was perfect, even if it was just for an hour or so over a cup of tea.

All I know for sure is that by allowing myself to be seen, open, and broken, and yet hopeful and determined to find a way beyond my brokenness, I became an instrument of change and healing. I transformed the falsity of the perfect life into that of the wounded healer. The wounded healer is that "no bullshit" person, the one who is genuine and authentic and not afraid to bleed and weep openly. The one who is filled with certainty and who moves forward living from her soul.

FEARLESSNESS

When I think of fearlessness I actually think that what we need to learn is how to be afraid, how to sit and accommodate that feeling and not run from it and also not be driven by it, because when we're driven by it we will do anything to avoid it. We will do things that are quite self-destructive or destructive to others, we will surrender good judgment; and if we could learn to sit quietly with our fear, surround it with awareness and love, then I think we will discover a whole new meaning of fearlessness.

— SHARON SALZBERG

Practicing fearlessness means having the courage to face the places within us where the Four Horsemen of the Apocalypse live. We carry within us ancestral and cultural stories related to the four figures in the Book of Revelation symbolizing conquest, war, famine, and death. We also carry all the stories passed down from our ancestors that are held firmly in place, pictures and objects that hold us in remembrance of these ancestors. Our deceased loved ones are now our ancestors too and, as we release the traumatic stories we carry about them, we lighten their memory.

Fearlessness does not mean you aren't ever afraid. It doesn't mean you don't have doubts. It means you decide to go forward anyway. I remember a story about a fireman on a ladder high up from the ground, coaxing a woman to come out of a window away from a burning building. The woman told him, "I can't do it—I'm too scared." The fireman told her, "Then do it scared."

Once my beloved son passed, it was as if I had been in a horrific car crash without my seat belt fastened. I was thrown out of the program, out of the Matrix. I landed hard, all my breath knocked out of me, and, scraped and torn and bleeding and near death myself, I saw everything in a different light. It was like a reincarnation within this lifetime. It took some time, but I began to see his death as a gift and an opportunity to change my life and do better for my daughter and friends and community. I was determined to make his death matter. I would do it scared.

An important part of my personal transformation process was letting go of several generations of collectibles passed on to me from my great-grandmothers, grandmothers, and mother. There were several antique cabinets full of china, silver, Depression glass, and Fiestaware—all the many sundry collections of several generations of women. It had been foisted on me by my mother and it had to stay in my house whether I liked it or not. Cake plates, punch bowls, and tiny coffee cups from a time when women served afternoon tea had never suited my lifestyle, and they had languished in my house for 30 years, the cabinet doors kept tightly shut to keep out the dust and keep the silver from tarnishing.

I chose a few mementos that were connected with happy memories and let the rest go. My daughter didn't want most of these things either, and I refused to pass on either the objects or the guilt associated with keeping them. I realized that guilty attachment to old ways and old stories and old things no longer served me or my daughter. My mother grew up during the Great Depression and lost both her parents at a young age. She never felt financially secure no matter how much money my father made, and her favorite saying was "Life is a bitter pill." Letting go of crippling anxiety around finances and her view of life was another step, freeing my daughter and me from any lingering attachments to ancestral stories and ties. Most of those stories were sad ones; the women of our lineage did not live happy lives. Letting the things go let the old sad stories go too.

I told my daughter to choose what she wanted and didn't guilt-trip her into taking the rest. She looked at me and said,

"Really? Are you sure you aren't mad?" The moment I looked her in the eyes and told her, "I'm not at all mad. It's important that you make your own choices," a familial pattern of manipulation by guilt seemed to float away, and the very air between us seemed to calm. Manipulation by guilt was how the women in our family seemed to operate. At that moment I knew we had freed ourselves from this destructive pattern. It was a big moment for both of us. We hugged fiercely, and from that time forward, we were able to ask each other, "What do you really want?" Our conversations became lighter as we allowed each other to live guilt-free.

I was advised to stay away the day of the auction when my house was emptied. But I did not cry as people came and took away things. I had already blessed them all and their journey to new lives with new people. Just like me, they had new and unknown destinies awaiting them somewhere in the future. Just like me, they could go there unencumbered by the weight of the past. New people to own them and love washing off the stale and sticky dust of the past that adhered to them. Maybe they would feel like I do after a morning shower, rinsing off yesterday and starting the day refreshed and renewed.

Just before the auction, my daughter came home to help me sort out Ben's room. It was just as he had left it, except for the clothing I had donated a few months after his death. I was filled with dread and not at all sure I could handle the rest. My daughter came prepared with boxes and large trash bags. Then she told me to get out and go shopping because she was going to take care of it all. And so I did. She asked me what I wanted, and I told her to pick a few things for me. As I said goodbye to Ben's room and left the house, I felt him sitting beside me in the car. I turned and asked him if it was okay. I heard his voice in my head saying, "It's better than okay, Mom. It's time."

Five weeks earlier, on the day I put my house on the market, I had made a mandala in my garden—an energetic circle under the sun and moon and stars made by calling in the archetypal forces of the four directions and heaven and earth. In the middle of the mandala I put a stone representing me and my little dog, Murphy, with the intent that our path forward be shown. I had just completed my shaman training a few weeks before I put my house up for sale. While I was there finishing classes, Alberto Villoldo, the founder of the Four Winds, asked me if I would be interested in working and training with them, starting out as an unpaid assistant in Chile.

I was ecstatic. I knew that this opportunity was in response to my wish for a life full of travel, meaning, and a spiritual path. It was far beyond anything I could have imagined for myself. By keeping my request simple, the universe filled in the details for me in a surprising and magnificent way. As soon as my house sold, I contacted my new employer and explained things were moving along rapidly and I would be available sooner than I thought. But weeks had passed, and I hadn't heard back. On the day of the closing, when I locked the door of my now-empty house behind me for the last time, I also closed my mandala, scattering all the elements of which it was made back to nature. As I walked away, I felt overwhelmed. I had a hotel room booked for a few days, but the rest of my life was open. It was a very strange feeling of disconnection. I had done it; I had ended my old life and I was teetering on the brink of something new. Fifteen minutes later I received a text message welcoming me to Chile and asking me to come immediately for an entire month.

Shamans are taught to learn to notice synchronicity all around us, and I knew that this timing was no fluke. This was Spirit answering the petition in my mandala at just the right moment. Yes, it might have been a bit less of a nail-biter if I had received the text a few weeks earlier, but I knew this to be a test of trust and faith. Could I leave planning for the future in the hands of divine forces? Did I really trust that I would be given the exact steps I needed to take at exactly the right moment? I could and I did.

All I know for sure is that letting go of the past, the stories, and the mementos set me free. When I realized that I was so much more than those stories, I stopped acting out of fear and a new life appeared. Synchronicities abounded and prayers were answered.

Exercises to Apply the Practices of the West Direction of the Medicine Wheel and Continue the Process of Transforming Our Lives

Begin by finding a notebook, a pen or pencil, a candle, and a small tin pie pan or tray. The pan will be used to catch ashes later in the exercise. In this exercise, you will write honest answers to four questions, then set an intent, hold them to the candle flame, and burn them. By burning them you release them to your concept of God, or Spirit, or Universe for your healing. Then allow your heart to open to allow in new ways of filling the newly freed space.

If you would rather light a fire in your fireplace or outside, that's fine too. In shamanic mythology, fire is a path of rapid transformation, so by burning your answers, you allow rapid transformation into your life. There's no need to worry that someone might find your answers because you will be burning them. This will allow you to be completely and radically honest in your answers because no one will see them but you.

Next find somewhere you can sit alone in stillness with your notebook, pen or pencil, candle, and pie pan beside you. Allow yourself this alone time when you have nowhere to go and nothing to do. As you sit, concentrate on your in-breath and your out-breath. When we breathe, we empty our lungs of old, stale air so fresh, new air can come in. Our breath is a metaphor for the exercises in this book. We are in the process of breathing out old, stale ways of being so new ones have space to live inside us. In solitude we can hear the voices inside ourselves that grow faint and are drowned out by the noise and busyness of our daily lives and by the presence of other people. Stay still until you are in a place of knowing that what you are hearing is the subtle voice of your spirit. Stay until the doors and walls you have erected around your broken heart are open. Once you feel ready, ask yourself the questions below and answer with radical honesty. That means no holds barred, nothing held back, courageously naming that which must be named for your transformation.

Ask yourself each of the following questions one at a time and immediately take your answer to the fire before moving on to the next question.

Ask yourself how you have conformed to the consensual in your life. Make a list of the cultural, familial, social, and professional conditionings that bind you, the ones you love, and the ones you don't. When you are finished, burn your list in your candle flame or fire with the intent of releasing conformity and conditioning and opening your heart to new choices.

Ask yourself what keeps you busy. What emotions are you avoiding by keeping busy? Make lists of both and take your lists to the fire. Burn your list of things that keep you busy with the intent of releasing the underlying fear of facing your emotions. When you are finished, burn the list of emotions you are avoiding in your candle flame or fire with the intent of facing them. Allow your heart to open to let nondoing and stillness come into your life.

Look at your life now and ask yourself whether you lost a part of yourself somewhere in the hectic rush of working, raising children, or taking care of elderly parents. Are there places in your life where you are not being open, genuine, and authentic? List the changes you would like to make in your life and the places you are wobbling about change and moving forward.

Next ask yourself whether there was a time when you felt you were in the flow of life, making choices based on what you wanted from life. Can you connect back to those choices and list what you wanted from life then and what you would like now?

When you are finished, burn your list of changes you would like to make in your life and your list of things you would like from life in your candle flame or in your fire with the intent of releasing uncertainty and wobbling. Open your heart to certainty coming back into your life, allowing yourself to be seen and available for change to occur.

Ask yourself how fear-based stories passed down through generations keep you from engaging fully with life. Are there fears that keep you isolated and alone? Are there family mementos that are holding pain and trauma? Are there family patterns of manipulation and guilt that keep you from making changes? Make a list and when you are finished, burn your list in your candle flame or in your fire with the intent of releasing ancestral trauma. Open your heart to new ways and a new life, even if it means "doing it scared."

CHAPTER FOUR

North Practices
of the
Medicine Wheel

Awakening

*A great traveler . . . is a kind of introspective; as she
covers the ground outwardly, so she advances fresh
interpretations of herself inwardly.*

— LAWRENCE DURRELL

In the North direction of the medicine wheel, we are in a place of possibilities and resurrection. A place of the seer who finds the longing of the soul. Like the tiny hummingbird anticipating its migratory journey flying high on wings of hope, we begin to feel the call of our soul for change. Letting go of heaviness in the South and West directions of the medicine wheel allows us to drink only from the sweetest nectar of life and make changes that honor our loved ones. Instead of being stuck in despair and hopelessness, we use the energy of grief and the wisdom we have found to create newness. We sense our loved ones cheering us forward. They, also, are resurrecting into their new lives on the other side. Our progress is their progress, and we move forward separate yet together.

Would I be able to step beyond the transformation processes of the South and West directions and begin resurrecting a new life? Could I let go of all preconceived notions and expectations, be in the present moment, approach life with curiosity and wonderment, and find my unique gifts and passions?

The practices of the North are beginner's mind, transparency, integrity, and living consequently. Looking at these four practices, I thought, *How wonderful! These are exactly what I need to resurrect myself out of hopelessness and despair and into a new life.* How have they worked for me?

Just as you did with the practices of the South and West directions of the medicine wheel, jot down anything you find relevant to your own life as you read my story. The exercises at the end of this chapter will help you work with your stories and the practices so you can begin the process of resurrecting into a new life from the ashes of the old.

BEGINNER'S MIND

When you allow yourself to be simple and quiet, in beginner's mind, you can experience your core motives . . . You're fine just as you are. Other people are welcome to see anything about you.

— PENNEY PEIRCE

The practice of beginner's mind involves releasing our notions about and expectations for life and welcoming new experiences with an eager heart and open mind. All of our past wisdom and experiences are part of what we bring to everything new, but we look through the eyes of a child to see the possibilities. We don't come from a place of "been there, done that," but look around in wonder, finding freshness and vitality.

Long before going to Chile, before even finishing my shaman training, I was invited by a friend to go to a psychic fair. I wasn't exactly sure what it was, but I was excited to go with her. My friend had a booth where she sold all sorts of crystals and gems. I was there to support her and was happily content to drift from stall to stall, each one containing something new and wonderful: a didgeridoo player warbling and wailing into someone's heart chakra, mediums and angel messengers, crystal merchants and tarot card readers. I took a moment to just stand at the end of an aisle and look around and take it all in. One old shaman caught my eye. He was dressed in buckskin and supported by a huge staff several feet larger than him topped with feathers.

In a room full of oddities, this old man had my full attention. And I had his. He limped straight toward me, each step preceded by the pounding of his staff and the shaking of feathers. Stopping right in front of me, he stared intently into my eyes. I felt him reviewing and analyzing me like I was a long and complicated Russian novel with many characters and a convoluted and twisted plot. I couldn't look away. Time slowed and then stopped; my surroundings disappeared, as did my awareness of my body. I was mesmerized. In this altered reality, the old shaman said, "You are filled with light and have much to offer." Then he turned and tippity-tapped away, the feathers topping his staff fluttering and flickering and cocooning his person and his passage.

I stood still in a timeless trance for a few moments longer, my nerve fibers, neurons, and synaptic junctions on alert, absorbing and interpreting. When the moment ended, I realized, as we sometimes belatedly do when time comes to a standstill, that I was blocking the crowded hallway. People were pushing past me and frowning. It was a glorious interlude and I felt refreshed and even blessed by the old man. As I walked on, still pondering, I heard a woman talking with her friends, saying, "I tried all of this stuff over the years and I can tell you that none of this stuff works." As the gaggle of gal pals giggled away, I thought maybe if she hadn't been so caught up in "been there, done that," she, also, might have experienced a glorious interlude.

I understood the concept of "been there, done that," and I was well acquainted with the attitude. After all, I lived in Washington D.C., and I was surrounded by well-educated and wealthy people. There was a lot of sniffing one's nose to indicate that the food wasn't as good as was experienced elsewhere, like New York, or the opera wasn't quite as good as when they saw it at the Met. It was a lot of posturing to prove one was cosmopolitan. Maybe it was because I came from humble beginnings, but it always seemed to me that this attitude really got in the way of enjoying the moment and kind of ruined experiences for others who in their enthusiastic enjoyment had revealed themselves to be country bumpkins. I never liked watching this attitude deflate people.

I often wondered about the old shaman telling me I was filled with light, but especially several years later when I was on the brink of collapsing my old life by retiring and letting go of my home and possessions. It seemed to me that the true test of my light might be whether I had also collapsed my old way of being? Could I let go of all of my preconceived notions, give up expectations, and live in the present moment? Could I approach life with curiosity and wonderment and be open and fresh to receiving new experiences? Could I be someone new?

I had cleared out the weighty stuff in my home, but had I been just as successful in clearing out my limiting beliefs? How much were old thought patterns still driving my decision making? Could I really reinvent myself and my world? Was I able to rest in the unknown, come home to Spirit, engage with my life as a lover, and be grateful for life and for each moment? These are the kinds of things that the saintly and reverent say. But I wasn't saintly or reverent, so could I move beyond these clichés to find some truth in those statements for myself? That seemed to be a really tall order, especially when applying beginner's mind to the very real choices and actions that pulled at my heartstrings.

One of the things pulling at my soul was my nine-year-old West Highland terrier, Murphy. Saying yes to Chile meant a month-long care plan because taking him with me wasn't an option. What I wanted to find most was a doggy sitter who would love him, be home during the day, and who didn't have other dogs. I didn't want to leave him in an impersonal kennel for a whole month—he hated being confined to a cage and made himself so sick the one time I had tried leaving him for a weekend at a "pet hotel" that I had to return early to pick him up.

As you can see, saying yes to a month in Chile was the first test. But there were more obstacles to face. How could I think about leaving Murphy for a month? And on top of that, what about my precious daughter? What if she needed me and I was half a world away? Even though I knew going to Chile was the right step forward into new beginnings, my fears implored me to reconsider! Fear shouted, "Stop this nonsense! Just take the easy way, the familiar path, and settle down, find a nice house in a new neighborhood, turn on the TV, and join the rest of the retired folks."

I looked at all those thoughts and realized they were all old, fear-based ways of seeing the world. I looked at all that had happened in such a short time—my retirement, selling my house and stuff, the call to come to Chile a mere 15 minutes after closing my sand painting—and knew the future was calling. With the winds of change pushing forcefully at my back, I decided I would be a fool to do anything but leap.

I had become very familiar with the tarot card the Fool. In most depictions, the Fool merrily walks along with only a bundle of belongings on a stick and the sun at his back. In front of him is a cliff. He either isn't looking or he doesn't care, and he's a few steps from walking right over the edge. The best part is the little white dog at his feet who looks a lot like my Westie, Murphy. One way to look at the dog is that he is barking to get the Fool's attention so he doesn't walk off the cliff. To me, however, it looked like the Fool's little white dog was barking merrily to cheer him along!

It occurred to me that I manufactured or perhaps summoned this guilt from my psyche purely to mask my fear of stepping off the cliff into the unknown. So I decided the guilt was not going to keep me back—I was leaping. Some might call me a fool for doing so, but I was getting accustomed to incredulous reactions. My daughter was an adult, living on her own, and financially independent, and did not need me close by. In this time of cell phones, Skype, FaceTime, and planes, we could connect in an instant, and I would be a 12-hour plane ride away at most. My daughter was fine. Murphy would be fine too and I trusted that the right doggy sitter for him would come along. Once I let go of the guilt dressed up as fear, the magic happened. A retired friend offered to take Murphy for the entire month I would be in Chile. She had no other dogs and would be home all day with him, and I knew she would be kind to Murphy. I was on my way!

It wasn't easy to leave Murphy even though I knew I had found the perfect place for him. The look of pleading in his eyes when I packed my suitcases and when my friend dropped me at the airport reinjured my grieving, broken heart. Saying goodbye to my daughter reinjured my broken heart. Driving away from my home of 25 years reinjured my broken heart. Leaving my friends reinjured my broken heart. I walked through the airport doors with a large, bruised, throbbing mass where my heart was supposed to be.

Just before getting on the plane, I received an e-mail from the airline company saying that my flight time had been changed. With all the packing and worrying, I hadn't read it carefully. I arrived at the bag check counter only to be told that not only had my flight time changed, but also the day! I was in shock. How could this be happening? I thought. How could an obstacle pop up when I was in the flow? I told the check-in clerk that I really needed to leave for Chile—everything was set up at the other end for my arrival and I needed to be there to assist with a class. She told me I could try to get on a later flight that day, but only standby was available and there were already seven of us on the list. It didn't look good. I decided to try to make the later flight anyway. I was nervous about my new position and didn't want to arrive late.

When I got to the gate I sat down and waited. I noticed several other people who were going back and forth with the gate agents, letting them know that they were on standby and really needed to make that plane. I watched one large red-faced man shout at the gate agent about how urgent it was for him to get on that plane and that he should get the first of any seats that came up because he had a very important meeting to get to. I watched an older woman ask whether she was going to make the plane, looking very frail and confused. I saw others stand and look anxious too.

As I observed, I began to feel the frustration, the fears, and anxieties of all those on standby swirl around me. And I began to feel overwhelming compassion for us all. Even for the loud, aggressive, and "important" man who was hoping to shout and threaten his way to the front of the line. I prayed quietly, "May we all make this plane; may no one be left behind. If someone must be left behind, let it be me." We all made the flight.

When I got to my seat, I thought, *Wow, I have changed.* The old me would have been one of those pacing anxiously, and I would have been glowering at the man who was trying to get in the front of the line because I, too, would be trying to be first in line! I would have been pissed off that he might beat me to it! I would have thought, *Who do you think you are? I'm not going to stand for your nonsense! You aren't going to push in front of me! I'm important too!* I would not have been able to sit still and observe, and I certainly would not have prayed for us all to make the flight or, if necessary, to be the one left behind.

It was an odd sensation of observing myself as though I were different parts of the same whole. Who is this person who is praying? Who is this person who is praying for everyone? Who is getting on a plane? Who is going to Chile? Who am I? I realized then that everything in me had changed. I had been reincarnated into a new life outside the tattered fabric of the old one. I was starting out fresh, weaving new threads into strange and unfamiliar designs. New ideas, new thoughts, new ways of being all weaving together into a brand-new tapestry.

I had been consistently employed for 30 years, even through childbirth, divorce, and death. It was a world that had felt safe and secure. Not only that, but I was in the enviable position of being at the relative top of my profession. Not many lawyers made it to becoming a judge. It wasn't the

Supreme Court, but it was impressive nonetheless. But now I was beginning anew and starting at the bottom. I was a novice shaman, still studying the complexities of energy medicine. I was entering a completely new world that emphasized perception and valued all those things my mother told me would put me in a loony bin!

My job in Chile was to be an assistant. This involved doing all the behind-the-scenes things that make a month-long class for 34 students and their teachers happen. One of my first tasks was to learn all about becoming a barista; running the fancy coffee machine and making fresh almond milk. I could barely figure out the TV remote in my old life. This was doggone challenging. The coffee machine had a lot of expensive breakable-looking parts, and not only did the almonds have to be soaked overnight and go through the blender but they had to be strained through cheesecloth so the fancy-pants coffee machine wouldn't get clogged. Needless to say, my barista skills were lacking in the beginning. Simply learning to strain almonds through cheesecloth was challenging, and a lot of almond milk was lost in the process! But I couldn't have been prouder when I figured it all out.

Alberto, my new boss, smiled watching me work. I had gone from judge to barista. Here I was in the beautiful mountains of Chile at a magnificent retreat center, living in a safari tent for a month. And serving coffee. I couldn't have been happier. I didn't even have this type of joy when I passed my bar exams on the first try.

Another part of my new job that I loved was readying breakfast protein shakes and supplements for each student. I rose in the chill of early morning in the mountains before everyone else, threw on warm clothes, and ran from my tent down a hill, across a small bridge, over a ravine, and up large stone stairs to the kitchen. This was much easier than conquering the coffee machine. I could handle counting pills and putting them in paper cups just fine, and figuring out how to make protein shakes in the blender went pretty well too. I had to laugh, thinking of what became of my Georgetown Law degree and all those years as a judge studying the financial reports of large corporations. It all added up to competency to count and strain almonds for homemade almond milk and become a barista! I thought that perhaps those were the best things I'd ever done with that law degree.

I was outside every day from the crack of dawn till the late hours of the evening. I ran from my tent up to the kitchen and classroom several times a day, and then up to the main house when needed. It was a lot of walking up and down hills. Much more than I was accustomed to doing. After a week or so I had lost some weight and I noticed that I was becoming more fit. All the walking was becoming easier and my steps were lighter. I fell into bed exhausted every night but with a song in my heart. I was serving the hearts and minds of others as I made coffee and counted pills and gave out hugs and listened with my open heart, and it mattered and was important.

Many people comment on how great my skin looks for my age, and I tell them it's because I rarely went outside for 30 years, driving from my home garage to my work garage and back again! I was profoundly sad that I had needed to confine myself so completely to do all that needed to be done to be mother, wife, daughter, and employee. If I had known then what death would teach me, I would have lived differently.

Although I was in the class taking notes, watching the teachers, and learning how to teach someday, the real lesson for me was not only learning to be of service but also *how* to be of service. My former high-powered job where people catered to me and my lifestyle of relative ease did not prepare me for a path of service. I didn't have the skills needed to know how to act or walk or breathe, or even just how to be myself. I didn't know this new me who was picking herself up from the ashes of the past. I didn't know how to connect with people in this new role. I didn't know the rules.

My isolationist ways and my avoidance strategies were useless. I had a roommate and I was surrounded by people 24/7. There was nowhere to run and no place to hide for an entire month. At first it was exhausting. I was accustomed to spending hours every week at a job where I could go in my office and shut the door. As a judge, people didn't often bother me. I could set meeting times to work with my law clerk and other staff as was convenient for me. I could spend days alone in my office working on decisions. It was a painful 30 days, learning to be present and available to students, teachers, the owners of the retreat, and other staff members. I was on call for everyone and had very little free time.

I had to look around and take cues from other people to see how they managed. By the end of the day, social interaction looked more to me like being assaulted. Sometimes it was painful. I needed to find my inner extrovert and keep her up and running. This wasn't an easy task for an introverted loner. I needed to either cobble together a new way of being or admit defeat. I looked everywhere for guidance—the teachings, the teachers, and everyone around me. I was running scared.

I didn't look within myself for answers because I didn't think I had skills worth recycling. Somehow when I lost Ben, I lost my confidence too. All the things I had held dear and thought were important to me had proven to have been illusions. I could only see my failures and how I could have done things differently. In this state of being, how could I trust anything within myself?

I loved my new assistant job as long as I was busy. But just keeping busy wasn't enough in this new role; I also had to learn to connect with people. When students come train to be a shaman, they often do so because they are in pain and in search of healing. I know I certainly was. But I wasn't a student; I was a staff member. A lowly one, to be sure. Nevertheless, students often turned to me to ask questions and to share their life stories, and I needed to be available. I needed to change.

My lifetime of insecurities all rose up in me with the vengeance of the living dead. They laughed the laugh of the demented, pointing their fleshless fingers at me and telling me I clearly had no skill for this new endeavor. They taunted me for throwing away my old life. They reminded me that I had become a laughingstock—someone who walked away from an enviable social and financial situation. But I didn't give in. I knew this was exactly where I needed to be. I needed to change my ways to grow and be resurrected into this new life. I needed to learn to open up and become available to people. I needed to become a healer. I wanted to become a teacher.

When evaluating my past life, it seemed to me that I was looking at what could be several lifetimes within my lifetime. There were my childhood and young adult years, my college years, my Army years, and my years as wife and mother, and now this new place of becoming a healer and teacher. I know that reincarnation in the traditional sense requires a physical death before resurrection. But it seems to me that parts of me did die after each of these life transitions. I know part of me died with Ben, leaving an open, raw, and tender space to fill. I knew that my old self, old thinking, and old ways of being had been transformed and new ways were coming.

I used that pivotal month to change. I opened up and allowed myself to become receptive and available to the needs of those around me. I lost the urge to run away from connecting with others and learned to enjoy interactions. I needed that month to become newly formed. I might never become a true extrovert, and I still love time alone. But I learned to value and even look forward to interacting.

All I know for sure is that death gave me the incentive and courage to begin anew, with distance from my old thoughts, beliefs, and safety nets. I knew I was beginning again in so many ways, and I knew that starting at the bottom in a completely new subject area, homeless and free from so many of the ties that bind, was perfection. I was the proverbial phoenix rising from the ashes once again. I was ready to fly! The only thing that could have stopped me was a circus elephant sitting on my chest.

TRANSPARENCY

We live in a culture of secrecy, where hiding and lying are accepted as natural, even though we don't like it. We want honesty, transparency, and authenticity in our loved ones, our groups, and organizations, and in our own self so we can reach the heights of our capacity. By clinging to the opaque reality we stall our evolution.

— PENNEY PEIRCE

The practice of transparency is one of allowing yourself to be seen in "all your perfect imperfections," as beautifully sung in the song "All of Me" by John Legend. Rather than hiding the parts of us we don't like, we allow our imperfections to be seen. Instead of hiding the parts of us that are wonderful but make others uncomfortable, we allow ourselves to shine. By allowing ourselves to be transparent, we also allow our authentic self to be revealed.

After assisting in Chile, I continued to travel and continued my shamanic studies. Another friend agreed to take my little dog Murphy for extended periods, freeing me to climb mountains in Peru, assist with more classes in Chile and California, and travel to Africa, India, Bangladesh, and the United Arab Emirates. I reveled in the beauty and mystery of Hindu temples, mosques, and Sufi shrines. But something was amiss with me that I tried very hard to hide from my fellow shamans and my friends.

I was physically ill with bronchitis and asthma, exacerbated from catching valley fever in California. I barely recovered from one bout of bronchitis before another came along. Nothing seemed to help. Also, my visions were getting stronger and I had less control over them. It seemed as if the sicker I got, the stronger the visions became. In Africa, lying in bed in my safari tent, I clearly saw a man and a woman dressed in blue sitting at the foot of my bed. Another time, I found myself at Ajmer Sharif, a Sufi shrine in Ajmer, Rajasthan, India, consulting with the revered Sufi saint, Moinuddin Chishti, about lifting a dark cloud around my daughter in Pennsylvania. I saw visions of enslaved people who had died in the slave market in Zanzibar and were stuck, who wanted my help to cross from this plane to the upper world, or heaven. I couldn't seem to control the visions any more than I could control the bronchitis.

It was important to me that my shaman friends saw me as strong and handling things well. After all, I was now an assistant teacher, so wasn't I supposed to be a model of control? And physical weakness was embarrassing to me. I was getting sick at moments when I was supposed to be teaching or in the midst of traveling with friends. Then there were the times I was with friends who weren't shamans or with my daughter. They could understand the bronchitis, but how could I explain my visions? I didn't want to worry or scare anyone. I knew I needed help, but instead I shut down.

I traveled to Peru twice during that time. I fell in love with the culture, food, textiles, and the beauty of the small towns and villages of the sacred valley. I traveled with a Four Winds group of shamans on a trip called Via Illuminata. We climbed mountains to sacred sites and joined in ceremony with Q'ero shamans native to Peru. The very air seemed different: the valley steeped with tradition and the echo of ancient footsteps of indigenous shaman and Inca rulers. The longings of my younger self to be an archaeologist and study anthropology made visiting the Sacred Valley and Machu Picchu special and enlightening.

The very air in the Sacred Valley is thin and clear, and the veil between the worlds is likewise thin and clear. I felt myself opening and relaxing into the ease of seeing clearly into the world on the other side. My customary mere glimpses of spirits in smoky glass, hearing and sensing the teachings of rocks and plants, and communicating with animals became as clear as when an optometrist examines your eyes and asks, "Which is better, number one or number two?" and you know immediately which one to choose. That's the way it was for me in the Sacred Valley—the sudden clarity was a relief in the sense that you don't realize how you were straining and tiring your eyes until you get new glasses.

By my second trip to the Sacred Valley, I had struggled with illness and uncontrollable visions for more than a year. So I wasn't completely surprised to wake up one night and see a luminous being standing beside my bed, filling the room with a shimmering, incandescent glow. I understood the meaning of the being as the light around it flickered and grew and then faded in intensity. The being told me that my soul shattered when Ben passed and that I must go to see John of God for healing. When I woke up the next day, I remembered vividly the visitation of the light being. It was different from any vision I'd had before, this time the vision came with a pointed instruction—I was told in no uncertain terms to go! I got up, looked up John of God healing trips, and booked the first possible guided tour, scheduled to begin in six weeks. I trusted and felt compelled by my imperious visitor.

John of God, or JOG, known in Brazil as João Teixeira de Faria or João de Deus, was then a recognized medium and psychic surgeon based in Abadiânia, Brazil, who ran a spiritual center, the Casa de Dom Inácio de Loyola. He did not claim to directly heal anyone but to physically incorporate various healing entities, mostly physicians who passed to him what people needed to do to heal. Thousands of people would line up before him, all wearing white clothing, asking to be healed.

Upon arriving in Brazil, I was hopeful that I could heal physically and spiritually at the Casa. I was with a tour group of 18 people and a guide. We flew into Brasília and spent a day there visiting the labyrinth and crystal pyramid at the Temple of Good Will, and then got on a bus for the two-hour trip to Abadiânia. The energy in Abadiânia was strong and vibrant, even in the streets around the Casa. People walked around dressed in white clothing, and the town was simple and clean. There was little loud talk or music and few loud cars. It had a sacred atmosphere.

The next day we went to the Casa and chose three issues we wanted the Entity to work on, and I worked hard to contain what I thought was the essence of my issues on the small square piece of paper provided. The Entity is what John of God was called when he embodied one of the healing entities around the Casa, or the doctors and healers from the other side. These entities brought along a whole phalanx of minor entities who were sent out to work on the 1,500 to 2,000 people who came through for healing every Wednesday, Thursday, and Friday, week in and week out.

Since the entities apparently only understood Portuguese, my issues had to be translated. In about 30 seconds, the translator had shortened my three issues to "grief," "bronchitis," and "spiritual problems." I gave a little huff of indignation, felt my eyes narrowing, and shot the translator a brief look of disgust. What the heck? I traveled all this way only to have my issues boiled down to four words! I believed there were a lot of nuances that were lost in this short and sweet translation. With a bit of a startle, the translator moved slightly away from me and assured me the entities could read my mind and heart and review my past lives. There was a long line of people behind me waiting for their translation. My allotted time with the translator was up and I had to move on.

The next morning, we woke up early to get to the Casa by 6:15 to get a seat. We were first-timers and the wait was long—about three hours. Finally, we were led before JOG sitting in Entity. Surrounding him were people sitting in "current." This is where hundreds of people volunteer to sit in meditative prayer, to keep the energy high in the room for those coming before John of God. We lined up and went through the "current" room approaching John of God one by one. He looked at each person for a few seconds and then he called out to a translator what each person required to heal. In my case I needed every healing modality offered at the Casa—crystal beds, an intervention (psychic surgery), and a regimen of herbs that had been prayed over by the entities. Others got off with far less.

I had no idea what "crystal beds" meant—I found out that afternoon that there were rooms with a machine with seven crystals attached. There was a massage table in the room, and when I lay down on the table, the crystals were adjusted to point at my chakras. When the machine was turned on, lights vibrated the crystals. I was to lie there for 20 minutes. I found it to be very relaxing and decided to schedule two more crystal bed sessions that afternoon.

The next day at 6:30 A.M., I was back at the Casa, this time in what is called the intervention line. This line was for those who had been prescribed psychic surgery by John of God the previous day. A long line of several hundred people moved through "current," past JOG, and into a room filled with long benches. We were instructed to close our eyes and sit with our right hands over our hearts. While in that room, each person was assigned one of the healing entities to work with us on our three issues. I looked around waiting for the action to start. I figured someone would say "Go!" and that I would then see hundreds of entities filing into the room. I saw JOG come into the room and briefly say something in Portuguese, then a staff person came and said something else in Portuguese. Much to my disappointment, I did not see entities filing into the room, nor did I sense or see any personal entity assigned to me.

Around 9:30 A.M., we were sent to our hotels in cabs to rest for 24 hours. I was to stay in my room with my eyes shut. No Internet, TV, reading, or staring at the ceiling. Our meals were even brought to us. I wasn't sure what to expect, but since I had not seen any entities in the intervention room, I thought that the 24 hours might be maddening. Nothing to do and nowhere to go—really? Surprisingly, it was very restful, and my thoughts seemed to be guided to old memories in a very gentle way, showing me how past events had deeply affected me. Looking at them seemed to allow me to release the power they held over me.

Around 4:30 in the afternoon I felt a presence in my room and suddenly felt severe abdominal pain. I saw a vision of a tall dark-haired young man at the side of my bed, bending over and peering at my lower abdomen. He seemed to be holding a very long and shiny knife. He said his name was Julio De something—a long name that I immediately forgot. He told me he died on May 16, 1920, and was a doctor. It seemed perfectly normal to me at the time to be speaking to a vision of a long-dead doctor. I said, "No disrespect intended, but you have been dead almost one hundred years, and we now have something called anesthesia. Are you, like, up-to-date with medical knowledge?" He was sweet and seemed to be quite a young doctor. He laughingly explained that all the entities are up-to-date and even beyond current medical practice. He said I had to feel the surgery so I would believe it happened.

He correctly diagnosed my skeptical tendencies! After he left, I slept on and off, feeling a lot of abdominal pain. Early the next morning, around 5:00 A.M., the same entity appeared in my room to check on me. I groggily managed to protest that abdominal surgery was not on my list of things to be worked on. He said it wasn't something I asked for but something I needed. Before I could get it together to ask what exactly it was that I needed, he flitted off. I tried calling him back, but apparently my allotted minutes to connect with him had expired.

My 24 hours in my room had ended too. I got up and noticed that I was bleeding vaginally. That hadn't happened to me for years. It occurred to me with great shock that it was the result of the psychic surgery. Something had happened; something was taken out or fixed in some way. So what about my list of three things—would those also be resolved? I was intrigued.

Forty-eight hours after surgery, we were allowed to go to the Casa and sit in "current." I could now be one of the volunteers sitting on benches praying as new lines of wounded people went before John of God, hoping for miracles. Dressed all in white, I arrived at the Casa again at 6:30 A.M. to stand in line and wait for the doors to open. The lore was that the adjacent room was where negative energy was taken out by entities and the JOG room was where you were attuned to higher frequencies. Those of us who were there to sit in current for the first time were advised to start out by sitting in the adjacent room.

But I knew where I wanted to sit—I wanted a front-row seat in the room where John of God sat. I wanted to see him channel and incorporate these healing entities into himself, and watch them take over his body! These entities bring with them numerous other entities who participate in the healings. JOG mainly channeled Dr. Oswaldo Cruz, a Brazilian physician, bacteriologist, epidemiologist, and public health officer, and the founder of the Oswaldo Cruz Institute; Saint Ignatius de Loyola, the patron of the clinic; and Dr. Augusto de Almeida. The JOG room was filled with huge crystals and statues of the Madonna, Jesus, Saint Rita, and others I might have recognized if I had paid any attention in Sunday school. There were also 13 high-backed chairs—6 on one side and 7 on the other side of the aisle leading up to the central chair where JOG sat. I supposed this was invocative of the 13 disciples around Christ. I remember reading that Oprah Winfrey sat in one of those 13 chairs when she visited the Casa.

As people milled around trying to decide what to do, I walked right up to the front and parked myself on one of the pews like I belonged there. I looked like a regular: I had a pillow for my back and a white blindfold to help keep my eyes shut. I found myself eyeing the 13 chairs in front of JOG, some of which were empty. I considered whether I could get away with plopping myself down in one of them, but that seemed too bold, even for curious me.

I wiggled and stretched and adjusted my pillow and blanket several times to settle in for a lengthy three- or four-hour meditation session. Even though I brought a blindfold with me, my intent was to keep my eyes open, watching everything until the last moment possible or until one of the proctors patrolling the rooms made me shut them. I noticed a monk in red robes who sat down in one of the fancy chairs, closed his eyes, and seemed to already be meditating. He didn't even have a pillow! Well, I huffed as my legs started to twitch uncontrollably—he had had more practice!

I had never in my life actually sat and meditated for three or four hours and never had the slightest desire to even try. But now, based on my ulterior motive to spy on the process, I was motivated. I wasn't entirely sure I would last the entire time, but I was assured that if I raised my hand, one of the nice volunteers would come and usher me out. Fantastic!

Once, I had signed up for a daylong meditation session at a Buddhist temple. It seemed like that was what spiritual people did to become mindful and be in the present moment. Even though I had never mastered even five minutes of consecutive meditation without my mind bouncing around frantically like a bee in a bottle, I decided to ramp things up. I wanted to be one of those spiritual people, so I thought I would try out a full day of meditation. I thought that by being surrounded by others meditating for hours, meditation skills were sure to rub off on me.

I was assigned a spot on the floor with a thin cushion at around 8:00 in the morning. We were instructed on how to sit and how we were to stay focused and not let our minds wander off. We would meditate for an hour and see how things were going. That was the longest hour of my life. My butt hurt, my back muscles had fully contracted, and my legs were twitching. I didn't get much out of the postmortem because I was fully focused on stretching my body. Before I knew it, meditation started up again. It was mind-numbing torture. I began to plot and plan ways to leave without offending all the really nice Buddhists. I thought a good story about an upset stomach and diarrhea would do nicely.

The gong sounded again, and just as I began to rise and peddle my story, it was announced that the next meditation would be a walking meditation and then we would have lunch. This was great news! I looked over the lunch buffet during the break and decided that Buddhists really had strange notions of lunch. No chocolate, no desserts, no pizza—nothing worth sticking around for. But I had a new escape plan. I joined the walking-meditation line with my arms folded just like the others, and as we shuffled past the cubbies where our shoes were stored, I furtively grabbed mine and made a beeline for the exit.

Since my aborted attempt at a daylong meditation, I had confined myself to gradually working my way up to a meager 10 minutes. But here I was again, looking at several hours of sitting quietly in meditation. At least we weren't sitting on the floor. We had wooden pews with backs and were allowed to bring in pillows and blankets and even eye masks if we had trouble keeping our eyes shut. There were many staff at the Casa making sure everything ran smoothly—ushers, people who lead prayers, translators, and people who watch over those who were sitting in current, making sure everything was okay and eyes were shut to prevent volunteers from seeing energies and entities being removed from people in line. Since that mostly happened in the room beside the one where John of God sat, I wasn't too worried. As I sat angelically in my seat, sneaking peeks from time to time from under my eye mask, prayers were being said in preparation for the arrival of John of God, the entities he incorporates, and the long line of people seeking healing.

During the prayers, I noticed one of the staff ladies placing a very large long-stemmed red rose on a three-foot-tall statue of Saint Rita holding a cross. Saint Rita was the patron saint of JOG and had been a very big deal at the Casa. The lady with the rose must have thought the cross was attached to the Saint Rita statue, so she prayerfully kissed the rose and dropped it onto the cross. Bam!—the cross sailed through the air and did a triple backward somersault before landing on the floor with a loud THWAK! At the same time, the rose flew in the other direction and landed beside the feet of the monk. I saw him open his eyes in shock and thought, *Ha, so much for Mr. Perfect Meditator.*

Now I was thankful I saved myself from trying to grab one of those fancy chairs—I was being rewarded for being so virtuous. Clearly, it was best for me to be farther back away from all the breakables! As I tried once more to settle in for the duration, I thought to myself that it was a good thing this happened before JOG and the entities arrived for the day. No telling what a bunch of entities ticked off by the assault on Saint Rita might do! I peeked over at the monk to see what he was up to, but of course he was already back in his zone. Show-off.

When JOG arrived at the Casa, the current room became highly charged. We were told to imagine divine light coming down through our crown chakra, through to the earth, and back up again, and out though our hearts. We were instructed to keep our hands, legs, and feet uncrossed, and told that by keeping our eyes closed, we would have less of a chance of picking up any negative entities released by the people coming through the line. As the shuffling and small movements of people settling in ceased and the 13 chairs were filled, the energy around us became dense and colors appeared under my closed lids, golden and rosy hues that swirled.

Even with my eyes closed, I felt the vibrations and saw the colors of the energy shift and change. The air before me became incandescent. It glowed and glittered and began to shimmer with the same lovely golden and rosy hues. As the chanting progressed, multihued lights glittered and glinted into the room. The ceiling was gone, replaced by what appeared to be stratums of clouds through which the lights entered. The air seemed to condense, and I found it difficult to breathe. The vibrations intensified and my ears filled and began to ache. I shivered and my skin was covered with goose bumps. I was on alert—something was coming. I longed to stay, but the urge to flee was strong.

As I watched the lights rain down, some emanations seemed familiar and pulsed with an energetic glow that surpassed the others. It seemed to me that they must be timeless spiritual masters who had ascended. Thousands of other lights appeared among them that also pulsed and shimmered but with less resplendence, touching someone here, hovering around someone over there, swishing and whirling, blessing and healing.

As I sat in current, JOG entered the room. He was said to be a powerful full-trance medium who could wholly incorporate different healing entities into his body. I wanted desperately to watch—I suppose the skeptic inside of me had to see it to believe it. Momentarily opening my eyes, I saw staff supporting John of God for a few minutes while a filmy white light enveloped him. He then sank into his chair. From where I was sitting, the incorporation was seamless except for making JOG appear to be a bit weak, leaning heavily on his aides. Other lights came into the room and surged and whirled among and around those seated in current. I decided to close my eyes as they flowed, touching and probing, lifting darkness and purifying the atmospheric essence.

As the line of people entered the room to see JOG, the entities engaged with them, extracting negativity and bringing healing so that by the time they reached JOG, people had already received some clearing. Our job in current was to keep the vibration of the room high and at a level where the entities could exist. I could no longer sustain my awareness of the room and I vibrated into an unconscious dreamlike state. Perhaps it's best described as a trancelike state of awareness but also unawareness. Four hours later awareness returned, and I noticed my back and legs were stiff.

JOG had disincorporated and the entities were gone. My awareness shifted to consciousness and I became cognizant of instructions given to me in my trancelike state. I was shown the charge of emotional energies. On one hand were the lower energies of sadness, despair, depression, and anxiety. On the other were the higher energies of love, joy, and gratitude. I was given a life review of my emotional states and the choices those states created around me, either limited and fear-based ones or limitless, creative, and joyful ones. At every juncture I had made the choice to go to the dark or to the light. The choice was and always had been mine. It was a simple yet powerful revelation. Although I sought the light, my yearnings were often overtaken by dark impulses arising from my subconscious to pull me down into old patterns and behavior. I was told to choose the light, day by day, week by week, until there was no more choosing, only a state of being in gratitude and joy.

But what about my three issues: grief, bronchitis, and spiritual problems? After my intervention I had another bout of bronchitis and I fell into deep doubt and despair. The vision of choosing seemed an empty one. How was I choosing illness and how could I transform grief? One morning as I walked to the Casa to meditate, a woman I didn't know and hadn't seen before, dressed all in white, looked directly at me and said, "Bronchitis is a result of deep grieving—they are connected. As you learn to live with your grief, your bronchitis will go away." I was shocked. How did she know about me? How did she know I had bronchitis or grief? Who had told her? I described her to others in our group, but no one knew her. I heard she had been coming to JOG for many years and often surprised people with such revelations. She was tapped in.

Later that day I introduced myself to a man in a motorized wheelchair who likewise had been coming to JOG for many years and who always seemed to be surrounded by people. I was told he had lived in Abadiânia since 2001 at the request of John of God and was full of wisdom and healing energy. I thought I would just say hello and move on by. It wasn't my nature to ask for help or open up readily to a stranger. He looked deeply into my eyes and asked what I needed to heal. I found myself talking about Ben and the deep grief I was carrying around. I asked him what I could do to heal myself because I couldn't seem to find the way.

He looked at me and said, "But you have found the way. You are writing and teaching, and touching people. These are blessings you were given—to learn how to live and love with grief and to show others the way. This is your way beyond grief. You are ready spiritually, and you have much to do here. Remember the other blessings you were given here at the Casa to clearly see how your choices raise or lower your vibration, and begin to consciously choose light emotions of love, gratitude, joy, and most of all hope. In that vibration your physical illness cannot survive."

"But what about my so-called spiritual problems and the visions?" I asked him. "I don't seem to be able to control them, and I'm embarrassed about that and about being physically ill all the time. Even here, I came with a group of 18 people and I'm the only one who ended up seeing and talking to an entity. How am I supposed to fit in somewhere? I always feel different, and I feel like hiding from people. I feel very alone, even with my shaman friends." He looked at me and said, "You have been given the gift of sight so you can help others to heal. You have felt its power and you felt it was out of control because you wanted to turn away from it and suppress it. When you embrace this rare and beautiful gift, you will find people that will not only accept you but celebrate you."

People come to the Casa broken and bleeding, physically and mentally, and unable to feel love, joy, and gratitude, but they leave with physical, emotional, and spiritual changes. Hope is powerful and carried all of us to the Casa. Hope carried me through all the days at the Casa, even when in doubt, and hope brought me to the right people at the right time. Hope is the bridge between the dark and light emotions, the way to joy, gratitude, appreciation, and love.

When I left Abadiânia, I had changed. Before, I was blind to the link between my grief and my physical health, and I was blind to the beauty of the gift of sight. I could now see how all the pieces fit into a perfect divine puzzle. I wanted miracles and I got them in ways I could have never foreseen. I left the Casa feeling the winds of destiny once again strongly pushing me forward. Will I stumble and fall and occasionally forget to choose the light? Probably. But I received powerful messages and interventions that I will not forget. When I returned home, I began to work diligently on this book so I could help people find their way through grief. In so doing I also found my own way. As I found my way emotionally, I healed physically. I no longer have bouts of bronchitis. I've stopped hiding my visions and worrying about fitting in. I don't reveal all that I see to everyone, but I have found a community that loves and supports me, and I feel so blessed to be able to help others with healing.

All I know for sure is that when I stopped hiding what I felt and sensed around me and became transparent and authentic, doors began to open. Some people still think I'm crazy, and I'm okay with that. Clinging to my fear of being different and not fitting into a mold had locked me down and stalled my own personal evolution for 30 years as I clung to the concept of success at any price. That fear had jammed me again, literally making me ill for several years after Ben's death. Allowing myself to be entirely seen helped me to achieve greater heights as a healer, reach more people than I ever could have imagined, and find a community that supports me. Travel had become a pilgrimage; I was no longer just running away from home.

Author's Note

I was horrified and blindsided when I learned about the accusations of rape, sexual abuse, and pedophilia against John of God by many women. The accusations led to a conviction. I support and sympathize with the women, and by telling my story, I am not advocating for JOG nor endorsing him in any way. My intention is to share the help I received from the spirits attached to the Casa and from the people who reached out to me while I was there. I believe that some background of my time at the Casa will help the reader understand my story.

INTEGRITY

Achievement of your happiness is the only moral purpose of your life, and that happiness, not pain or mindless self-indulgence, is the proof of your moral integrity, since it is the proof and the result of your loyalty to the achievement of your values.

— Ayn Rand

The practice of integrity is one of being true to your word and accountable for yourself and to others. Sometimes it's relatively simple, like going out with a friend as promised even though you would rather stay home and read. Then there are the more difficult promises and commitments we make to work projects and our families and friends. And finally there are those times when we must honor commitments we made to ourselves. Sometimes honoring commitments to ourselves can seem the most difficult. It may mean that we cannot go forward living someone else's dream no matter how enticing. It may feel uncomfortable to realize we cannot worry about disappointing anyone but ourselves. Searching our hearts we begin to see our own way forward.

One such moment stands out clearly for me. I had just completed all four directions of my shaman training. I was elated and on the threshold of making several big decisions. I loved the healing traditions of the Andean shamanism I had learned, but I was also interested in the Lakota traditions. I was introduced to the Lakota traditions in shaman school when I was assigned a roommate at a retreat center in Massachusetts while we were studying the South and West directions of the medicine wheel.

When I registered for the class, I very clearly stated that I wanted a private room, but upon arrival I found myself assigned to a double cabin with a broken heater. I had just had my right hip replaced a few months earlier, and I was experiencing a lot of pain. I had trouble walking and especially sitting on the floor. I surely was not a happy camper and wallowed in my own misery. I wanted to go home at the end of the day to my own space, and I was not at all interested in welcoming a roommate and having forced interaction outside of class.

However, this ended up being another part of my awakening. I was given the best roommate possible for a miserable, cranky, pain-filled me: a cheerful, optimistic woman from Alabama with a big personality and a deep Southern drawl. She had also been a judge and had retired, and she had recently suffered the death of her husband. One of her gifts was seeing the best in people and bringing it out. We bonded over our recent mutual losses. We both had had contact with them from the other side after they passed, so we could also share that very special relationship. It was just what I needed but didn't know it—long and meaningful chats with a roommate who understood me and who could and did help me along my new path.

My roommate had traveled a spiritual road with the Lakota tribe for more than 30 years. She is a Lakota pipe carrier and a tribal elder with her own lodge. A pipe carrier is someone revered and acknowledged in the community as a healer with spiritual gifts. The pipe itself is a sacred object, and the smoking of the pipe is a sacrament between humans and the sacred, as well as a means of communication and healing. She, too, had wanted a private room, but Spirit had put us together, and we formed a lasting friendship.

She invited me to come to her lodge and sweat with the community near Cooperstown, New York. I made several trips there, and when it came time for my vision quest, I decided to do it in the Lakota tradition. I loved the community and the symbolism of the sweat lodge, with the masculine fire and hot stones being brought deep into the sacred feminine of the lodge for healing.

Vision quests are part of shamanic training and a way of deeply connecting to the spirit world. It is a sacred time of seeking answers and guidance from Spirit. I prepared for several months to spend three days on a mountain in West Virginia, a sacred place of protection welcoming vision questors seeking refuge on its soil and beneath its trees. There were two others who were vision questing at the same time I was.

During the three days of fasting and prayer we hoped to prove ourselves worthy to receive from Spirit the answers we sought. I wanted to know what to do next: Should I involve myself deeply in the Lakota tradition, perhaps volunteering on a reservation? Or should I continue training as a shaman in the Andean tradition? Or was there another, entirely different spiritual path for me to pursue?

The vision-quest process required months of preparation, including six sweat lodges, fasting one day a week, and preparing a quilt with an eight-sided star. One of the few things you could take up on the mountain for protection was a quilt onto which the eight-sided star had been stitched. When I was shown an eight-sided star, I recognized it immediately. Thirty years earlier I had made one in a quilting class. It was the one and only thing I made, and I had kept it all these years, packed away on a shelf. I couldn't have told you why I kept the star all those years until then. I remembered my 30-year-old self sewing the star and feeling it was powerful but not knowing why. Now I knew I had been preparing my future self for this vision quest.

Vision questing with the Lakota is a big community event. Vision questers are special because they have been purifying themselves for months in preparation for asking Spirit for guidance. The community comes together to support the questers in many ways. Special places are prepared on the mountain for each quester. A sweat lodge is prepared with all the people who make the lodge possible—the fire keeper, the fireman, the lodge leader, and the one who pours the water. During the vision quest, the fire is kept going day and night to "feed" those on the mountain who are fasting. The community comes together mornings and evenings to sweat and pray for the vision questors.

Each quester also asks for two supporters to help with preparation and to pray for them while they are on the mountain. I was lovingly wrapped by my supporters in layers of the feminine. One supporter traveled from California and one from Arizona to be with me. With great excitement we packed my car full of clothes, food, and supplies, and set forth on the five-hour journey to West Virginia. I was nervous and excited. While talking and driving, my thoughts were focused on my vision quest. I already felt the mountain calling to me; it was vast and imposing, beckoning me forward with the promise of unfolding many mysteries.

I imagined sitting alone on the mountain for three days, watching the sun rise and set, and gazing at the patterns of leaves rendered by trees against the changing colors of the sky and the passing of clouds hour by hour. I thought of the days and nights of dreamily following the flight of birds, listening to the sounds of insects and the rustling of animals, and having time to observe the colors of sunset followed by twilight and ultimately complete darkness. It was the darkness I feared most. What would it bring? Wildlife or otherworldly life? Revelations or recriminations from the spirit world? I knew it was the darkness that would speak to me.

Several hours into our drive, as we turned off the main highway, a baby deer darted in front of me. I slammed on my brakes and missed the baby, but the mother was right behind it and she slammed into the side of my car, smashing the driver's side and bending the frame into the tire. My car ground to a halt. The impact threw the mother deer backward onto the side of the highway. I could see her struggling to get up, but her legs were broken. My friends and I were in shock. I began to wail for the mother deer and for her baby. I was beyond comfort and none of us knew what to do. The road was deserted, and we were without cell phone reception.

At that moment I wanted to turn around and go back home. This felt like a warning to stay back. But my supporters had come a long way and a supporting community of

20 people as well as the other 2 vision questers were waiting for us on the mountain. Even though it felt like a bad omen, I wanted to make it to West Virginia. I had prepared for months, and the community only got together once a year for this big event. If I didn't make it there now, I would have to wait another whole year. Fortunately a friendly soldier from a nearby reserve unit stopped to help us. He pushed my car off the road and he put the mother deer out of her misery by shooting her with a pistol he carried in his car. He called a tow truck for us and drove us to get a rental car. The arrival of this good Samaritan was confusing. It seemed like a good omen. Did this cancel out the bad omen?

An hour or so later, we arrived at the camp. I was pale and shaking. I couldn't get past the sight of the dead mother deer lying on the side of the road, and I worried about the motherless baby. I felt it was a message of some kind, hovering at the edge of my mind and nagging at me. But everything was in place: the sweat lodge, the fire that would be tended night and day, and the food and lodging for everyone. I sat with my two supporters, completing one last task—making prayer ties, 108 little pouches filled with tobacco. Each color represented the colors of the Lakota medicine wheel: red, green, yellow, and white. They were tied together with red string, so when we finished, we had one long rope of 432 prayer pouches, 108 for each of the four directions. This rope would go up the mountain with me and surround all four sides of the small space that had been prepared for me there. The space was just large enough for me to lie down, and I was to stay within its confines for all three days. The prayers were for my protection and to show me to be a daughter of the Lakota, seeking a vision.

That night delicate tendrils of mist seemed to come and wrap around me, binding me to my commitment and calling me to the mountain. The next morning, I dressed in white, and my supporters gathered my quilt with the eight-sided star and my prayer ties and walked me up the mountain. I sat in my small space surrounded by my prayer ties with my quilt around my shoulders. It was a beautiful July day, and it passed just as I had imagined: morning crispness changing slowly and lazily into the warmth of a sultry summer day. The sun moving overhead inevitably across the sky, making its way slowly over the horizon, turning day to dusk and then eventually into night. I was afraid of the dark as a child and always slept with a nightlight. I still wasn't entirely comfortable in the dark, and that night, with the winds rustling the leaves, I couldn't help but wonder what was around me. It was terrifying to not be able to turn on a light to see whether it was a bunny or a bear making those noises. And I couldn't leave—I had no idea how to make my way back down the mountain by myself, and besides that they had taken my shoes! Clearly, they had me tagged as a runner. My courage fled and I wondered how I could have ever thought this was a good idea!

A vision quest is a rite of passage for a shaman, culminating years of training. It is a sacred commune with the spirit world, bringing greater connection and messages. Preparing for the vision quest and sitting for three days without food or water shows our humility. We are willing to deprive our bodies in submission to the great vastness of the universe. We ask for guidance, showing great respect and deference. And, most important of all, underlying our asking is our pledge to honor the guidance Spirit gives us. Being in integrity means that we honor both parts of this agreement.

While I believed in my heart that three days of fasting and my humble request for guidance would put me in touch with messages from the spirit world, sitting in the dark on the mountain by myself, I couldn't help but think that I could have done it on my own back porch, with doors and windows closed and locked! What seemed to be a courageous and wonderful experience from the safety of my home suddenly seemed foolhardy.

Yes, there was an entire community of people down the mountain praying for me and the other vision questers, but I couldn't hear or see them from up where I was. And if I screamed, they wouldn't be able to hear me either. *Why, oh why did I have to romanticize this adventure?* The rustlings seemed to move behind me, then to the right, and then to the left. I looked frantically around, trying to make my eyes see into the darkness for hours. Nothing jumped out and grabbed me, so I had to trust that perhaps those prayer ties around me really did work as I fell over into an exhausted sleep.

Sometime during the deep velvet darkness of the night, I awoke to a loud rustling sound beside me and an awareness that I was no longer alone. The shadowy shape of a deer glided over and hung, suspended, near my right side. It was a dark shape but also translucent. A floating see-through deer—awesome! I knew it was the deer that I killed on my way. And then it began to speak—a floating see-through deer that talked—just great! It said, "The path of suffering is not your path. We tried to stop you. The path of the shaman will provide the wisdom you seek." Then the floating, talking see-through deer slowly evaporated. Surprisingly I wasn't terrified and immediately fell over, asleep. Perhaps I was in shock. I woke up feeling very groggy and nauseated. It was early morning and pink and orange rays were lighting the horizon. I found myself lying about 20 feet from my prepared spot and prayer ties, as if I had been pulled out and dragged away.

I was terrified, trying to figure out how I had gotten there. I didn't remember anything after the talking deer and being told the path of suffering was the Lakota path and not for me. My path was the path of the shaman. I had a feeling that hitting the deer on the way to my vision quest was an omen, but I hadn't listened to my instincts telling me not to go up the mountain, to go home. Had I known that deer medicine was the medicine of the Lakota chief hosting the vision quest, I might have listened. But perhaps not. I was inexperienced in the ways of omens and listening to my instincts. But by going up the mountain I not only got an answer from the spirit world to my quest, but also a lesson on observing and listening for answers given by the natural world. The deer had come as a potent messenger.

I love the Lakota path and the beauty of its ways. When I went through my friend's door to a vision quest, I had hoped this was my path to experience the divine, but it was not to be. Even though I was a lawyer and believed I could have helped defend water rights and do other legal work for the Lakota, the marked paths, the ones foot-worn smooth by many moccasins and lined with familiar faces, were not for me. I was profoundly disappointed. I didn't want to be a solitary pilgrim; I wanted to be part of a tribe, more precisely the Lakota tribe of my dear friend. I could have ignored the deer warning and pushed forward along the Lakota path. I tried telling myself that I was mistaken, I hadn't really seen the translucent talking deer and it was just a dream, but I knew better. Even though I loved the community and loving hands reached out to me, ignoring the message of the deer would have been living a lie and completely out of integrity.

I remember other times during the course of my life when I had made choices that were pleasing to someone else, or that conformed with social expectations, and wondered how things might have been different if I had followed my own path then. But it seemed to me that those past experiences gave me the wisdom I needed to heed the lesson from the spirit world here and now. The lesson of deer medicine was to step back from my old pattern of forcing life to be the way I wanted it to be and step into a new pattern of allowing Spirit to take the lead and show me the way forward. And that made all the difference.

All I know for sure is that the only way for me to move forward in integrity was to accept the deer message and follow the shaman path. As I let go of control and followed the shaman path, I found a life that was more fulfilling than I could have imagined. A life that brought me travel, friends, and a spiritual path that gave my life meaning and purpose and led me to the teachings and practices that are the foundation of this book. Although I didn't know it at the time, there was a divine plan for me, enabling me to live in integrity and write this book.

LIVING CONSEQUENTLY

Instead of obsessing about some traumatic or stressful event that you fear is in your future, based on your experience of the past, obsess about a new, desired experience that you haven't yet embraced emotionally. Allow yourself to live in that potential new future now, to the extent that your body begins to accept or believe that you are experiencing the elevated emotions of that new future outcome in the present moment.

— DR. JOE DISPENZA

Living consequently is an everyday, every moment kind of practice of monitoring our thoughts. Have we left the present moment to ruminate on old traumatic stories? Are we engaging in worry about the future because we fear repetition of past traumas or disappointments? The practice of living consequently is to concentrate instead on our wildest hopes and dreams and feeling the wonder and excitement of living and experiencing those dreams. We become aware of our old fear-based stories and consciously decide to put them aside and live our dreams.

Well, what the—? I'd been writing legal briefs and court decisions for 30 years, and when I first read the above quote by Dr. Dispenza, it sounded like bullshit to me, like some old saying my mother told me: "Be careful what you wish for. You just might get it." I got myself all twisted up trying to figure out whether something I thought or said or feared caused Ben's death. Or did Ben's fears create his death, or did we co-create it together? Did Ben want to die? Did he decide living was too painful, so he selected that future outcome? Did all my prayers for Ben over the years mean nothing because I prayed the wrong words or because I didn't do it Dr. Dispenza's way? I got mad at Dr. Dispenza; it felt like blame landing on me.

I loved the life I resurrected from the ashes of my old one. Teaching and traveling the world taught me a lot about myself. I could be a beginner once again and experience all the excitement of something mentally and physically stimulating. I became more open and able to reveal even the frankly freaky part of me that communicates with beings on the other side. I found the courage to walk my own path, even if it meant leaving the security of familiar people and places.

My Four Winds odyssey took me to places I had never been before: Chile, Peru, upstate New York, and even the high desert of Joshua Tree, California. I found that I liked interacting with students and teaching shamanism. I met hundreds of people who expanded my world way beyond what my limited thinking could conjure up. In search of mending my broken heart, I went on pilgrimages to Brazil, Spain, Germany, Switzerland, India, Bangladesh, Kenya, and Zanzibar. As I traveled I made new friends who became family and I grew in experience and wisdom.

At the point when traveling, teaching, study, and contemplation converged, I realized I was seeking answers to how to live with my grief. My reaction to Ben's death was extreme. I couldn't cope and I fled from my former life. But flight turned into an untethered seeking of answers that I knew by the lightness of my spirit were granted to me by all the powers that be. I sought a way to live life with a broken heart without avoidance or pretense. I sought and traveled and prayed for two and a half years until the wheels started falling off my suitcases.

I bought expensive suitcases, usually wandering around with two large ones and a carry-on so I could have clothes for every season wherever in the world I might find myself. Every now and then, I managed to fill my suitcases with exotic scarves and sacred tapestries, crystals, and carvings, and I would leave a suitcase at my daughter's house and purchase a new one. So I was a bit surprised when the wheels fell off one of my suitcases. I dragged the broken suitcase around an airport in Brazil, wondering where and when I would be able to buy another. Dragging a broken suitcase around an airport is not at all fun, especially when you have another big one and a carry-on in tow. It's not something you forget. Soon after I replaced that suitcase, the wheels broke on another one, again causing me to drag it around an airport. It occurred to me that something other than worn-out suitcases might be up, but I kept going.

When the wheels broke on a third suitcase just before Christmas in 2018, I was in an airport on Easter Island in the middle of the Pacific Ocean. I badly wanted to see the carved statues, the Moai, and soak up whatever wisdom they had to offer. My life had become a dance of one-way tickets to whatever destination seemed to call me. I didn't have definite plans, only opportunities. I could have hopped from

Easter Island to Micronesia to visit a friend. I could have flown back to Chile and spent some time in Patagonia.

By this time continual travel had become a way of life. There was always something to learn, some new sacred site to visit, and friends to connect with. But after the third suitcase demise, I finally got the message. I was being shown something profoundly important: it was time for me and my suitcases to stop frenetically traveling, and rest and regroup. So I booked a flight home to my daughter's house on Christmas Eve, arriving in time for Christmas and a loving invitation to stay as long as I wanted.

It was time to stop and reflect on my pilgrimage. What had I learned from the Moai in Easter Island, from the shaman in Kenya, from praying at temples and a Sufi shrine in India, from mosques in Bangladesh and the United Arab Emirates, from the entities and energies at the John of God Casa, from going around the medicine wheel time after time as I became an assistant and then a teacher? As I looked back on those travel years, I realized that I had been granted a boon. I had learned about the transformational power of grief. Each step along the way opened up before me, and then I was guided and prompted to stop. I knew that I had been given something precious, something to share.

I also knew it was time for something new in my life, but what? Help arrived in the form of my wonderful evolutionary astrologer, who was instrumental in setting me on my shaman path. This time he predicted that very soon I would be writing and teaching a class of my own. I was stunned by this prediction. He concluded this reading by asking if I was ready to embrace his predictions. I said yes! I didn't fully appreciate the power of it, but I now know that by saying yes, I was selecting the future for myself that included teaching and writing something of my own.

Teaching wasn't new to me. I had taught trial advocacy at George Washington University Law School in Washington, D.C. years ago, before Ben passed and I retired. And for the past few years I had been assistant teaching and then teaching shamanism. But I had never considered developing and teaching something of my own. I was intrigued, and the possibilities had me tingling. What if my life was once again about new beginnings? I held those possibilities in my mind like a secret treasure. I felt that sharing them would bring them into a world that would pounce on them and tear them to shreds with practicalities and limitations and obstacles. But if I kept them to myself, I could imagine all sorts of delicious opportunities.

For weeks after my astrology session, I envisioned myself on a stage teaching to large groups. I embraced being a successful author, and I desired becoming a loving teacher who helped people with grieving. I created a secret world that I could visit and paint with vibrant colors, people, and places. I could imagine myself in contexts and situations that I would have been ashamed to speak out loud to anyone. And I could sense the feelings of wonder and excitement and joy without shame or judgment. And as it turned out, feeling was the key to everything. Thank you, Dr. Dispenza—I'm not so mad at you anymore!

My journey began by asking myself a simple question about what I would like my future to look like. This question led to simple answers: traveling and finding how to live with my deep grief. These were founded in possibilities I knew I could figure out and make happen—probable possibilities. I could figure out how to retire, including a financial glide path; I could figure out places I would like to visit and where to stay when I arrived. And I had seen how it all had come to fruition with breathtaking speed. By simply saying yes and ignoring practicalities, limitations, and even common sense, I was able to make this simple future happen.

It was based on Newtonian concepts of the laws of physics and how the physical world operates. If $A + B = C$, then $C + D + E = F$. For example, "If I retire and sell all my possessions, then I will be able to finance traveling and living a full and interesting life." Or, "If I accept an assistant position with the Four Winds, then I can learn practices that will lead to living a full and interesting life."

But I had advanced beyond my initial simple dream of travel and finding how to live with my deep grief. My new dream, being a successful author and becoming a loving teacher who helped people with grieving, was based almost entirely on improbable possibilities! Yes, I am highly educated and yes, there are associative possibilities that I would be able to teach and write something. But the probability that I would step forward to write a book and teach a class was an improbable possibility. Writing a book and getting it published seemed impossibly difficult. And teaching a class would require structure and substance that seemed out of my reach.

So, dreaming about a new future felt like I was simply engaging in something that just felt good. Although I understood Dr. Dispenza's words, I hadn't fully embraced what the concept described. I didn't understand then that I was dreaming in a new and powerful way. To paraphrase Dr. Dispenza, I was living in that potential new future now, and my body began to accept or believe that I was experiencing the elevated emotions of that new future outcome in the present moment.

I was using principles of quantum physics in combination with something very ancient revealed in one of the Dead Sea Scrolls, the Great Isaiah Scroll, predating the biblical book of Isaiah by nearly 1,000 years. It was an ancient mode of prayer that involved feeling the desired outcome of your prayer in order to obtain the desired results. This mode of prayer is discussed fully by Gregg Braden in his book *Secrets of the Lost Mode of Prayer: The Hidden Power of Beauty, Blessing, Wisdom, and Hurt.* So even if the whole subject of quantum physics gives you a headache and leaves you cold, the concept of prayer might be comforting to you as it was to me.

Feeling our prayers and recognizing the wild and beautiful forces within us that we can tap into was exciting, and it motivated me to try it and see what I could create. As you pray, imagine how it would feel if what you were praying for already had happened. Pray and experience the joy and gratitude you would feel just as if your prayer had already been granted. My prayer was to live my passion of writing and talking to people about my journey with grief. I connected so strongly that I could feel the excitement of it all running through me and I was able to look to the sky and say thank you with all my heart.

All I know for sure is that I didn't fully realize the scope of what I was capable of creating. I didn't realize that I could take a quantum jump to create improbable possibilities—until I did it. I made a leap of faith, and unexpected and extraordinary things began to happen. I began to write this book and put together a podcast and a website. Friends and acquaintances reached out, putting me in touch with groups and organizations I had never known existed, and I began holding workshops. I finished putting together a course and finished this book. The improbable was happening all around me.

Exercises to Apply the Practices of the North Direction of the Medicine Wheel and Step into the Process of Resurrecting New Lives

Just as you did with the exercises at the end of the South and West directions, begin by finding a notebook, a pen or pencil, a candle, and a small tin pie pan or tray. The pan will be used to catch ashes later in the exercise. In this exercise you will write honest answers to four questions, then set an intent, hold them to the candle flame, and burn them. By burning them you release them to your concept of God, or Spirit, or Universe for your healing. Then allow your heart to open to allow in new ways of filling the newly opened space.

If you would rather light a fire in your fireplace or outside, that's fine too. In shamanic mythology, fire is a path of rapid transformation, so by burning your answers, you allow rapid transformation into your life. There's no need to worry that someone might find your answers because you will be burning them. This will allow you to be completely and radically honest in your answers because no one will see them but you.

Next find somewhere you can sit alone in stillness with your notebook, pen or pencil, candle, and pie pan beside you. Allow yourself this alone time when you have nowhere to go and nothing to do. As you sit concentrate on your in-breath and your out-breath. When we breathe, we empty our lungs of old, stale air so fresh, new air can come in. Our breath is a metaphor for the exercises in this book. We are in the process of breathing out old, stale ways of being so new ones have space to live inside us. In solitude we can hear the voices inside ourselves that grow faint and are drowned out by the noise and busyness of our daily lives and by the presence of other people. Stay still until you are in a place of knowing that what you are hearing is the subtle voice of your spirit. Stay until the doors and walls you have erected around your broken heart are open. Once you feel ready, ask yourself the questions below and answer with radical honesty. That means no holds barred, nothing held back, courageously naming that which must be named for your transformation.

Ask yourself each of the following questions one at a time and then immediately take your answer to the candle flame or fire before moving on to the next question.

Ask yourself what new things you have always wanted to do but were afraid to try. Be extreme—for example, maybe you are a librarian who always wanted to be an emergency medical technician. What did you want to be before duties and responsibilities took over? List them all and don't allow yourself to say, "I'll have to start at the bottom," or "I'm too old," or "The time has passed." When you are finished, burn your list in your candle flame or in your fire with the intention of releasing your fears. Then open your heart and invite new possibilities created from the energy of beginner's mind into your life.

Make a list of the aspects of you that you are hiding because you don't like them or fear them. Make another list of the aspects of you that are wonderful but you hide so you don't make others uncomfortable. Maybe your list includes seeing your departed loved one but fearing others won't understand. When you are finished, burn your lists in your candle flame or fire with the intent of releasing all that you are hiding. Then open your heart and invite in all your "perfect imperfections" so you can be entirely seen as you really are.

Ask yourself whether there are parts of your life you are living to keep the peace, to please someone else, or to live someone else's dream? What dreams would you love to create for yourself? When you are finished, burn your list in your candle flame or in your fire with the intention of releasing old ways of being that no longer serve you. Open your heart and invite in integrity and a new pattern of allowing Spirit to take the lead and show you the way forward to create your own dreams.

Do you have dreams that appear to be impossible or improbable? Ones that seem beyond your grasp or ones that require resources that you think you don't have? List all of them and sit with each one, and imagine how you would feel if your dreams came true. Imagine your excitement, joy, and gratitude. Imagine jumping up and down and pumping your fists with victory. When you are finished, burn your list in your candle flame or in your fire with the intent of releasing all that is holding you back. Open your heart and invite in your new dreams with gratitude and thankfulness.

CHAPTER FIVE

East Practices
of the
Medicine Wheel

Creating a New Life

To tap into the power of dreaming, we have to be connected not only to humanity. Our sense of oneness has to include the rivers and the trees and the crickets. Our story has to become large enough to include the stars and the galaxies.

— ALBERTO VILLOLDO, PH.D.

In the East direction of the medicine wheel is the way of the sage, where we become one with Spirit. We are at long last in a place of rebirth, a place of transcendence, where we find our calling and create for ourselves a new life filled with hope and joy and grace. The archetypal force is the condor or eagle, who flies wing tip to wing tip with Great Spirit, soaring high over the mountains and focusing on the big picture in ways in which we could only have dared to dream before death came to us. This is where I got in touch with the sage within, created a white canvas for Spirit to show me the next steps, and dreamed a new and fulling world reflecting an inner beauty I was finally able to embrace.

The practices of the East direction are no mind, no time, owning our own projections, and indigenous alchemy. How very esoteric these practices were to me, almost seeming to be luminous and ethereal. They perfectly reflected what I imagined Ben's rebirth to be. As with the practices of the South, West, and North directions of the medicine wheel, as you read with my story, jot down anything you find relevant to your own life. The exercises at the end of this chapter will help you work with your own stories and the practices so you can be reborn into a luminous and ethereal new life using all the wisdom of your grieving journey.

NO MIND

No thought, no mind, no choice —
Just being silent, rooted in yourself.

— OSHO

The practice of no mind is closely related to the practice of nondoing that we learned about in the West direction. Both practices get us in touch with our Observer Within, our enlightened nature that has never been born and has never died. With the practice of nondoing, we began to disengage from the distraction of busyness. With the practice of no mind, we disengage even from the distraction of our own thoughts. You start to notice your thoughts jumping around in your head with amusement and detachment. Once you ask yourself, "Who is it that is thinking these thoughts?" and then find the Observer Within, you become open to everything and you begin to act from a place of wisdom. You become a sage.

Not only had the wheels fallen off my suitcases, letting me know it was time for me to stop traveling, but also my long-term dog sitter of two and a half years was moving and could no longer take care of Murphy. I needed to find a place for both of us to live. When I stopped traveling and arrived back in the U.S. at my daughter's house, I was tired and jet-lagged and a little scared. I had a clear direction and a sense of purpose and meaning but little else. So many practical questions were running constantly through my head. The end of ceaseless travel meant I needed to find somewhere to live. During my travels I had entertained the notion of building a house in Chile or renting and living long term in the Sacred Valley in Peru. But everything changed when I found out I was to become a grandma. My baby girl was having a baby; it was extraordinary to me. Of course, she was all grown up but she will always be my baby girl.

I love my daughter fiercely and love spending time with her, but neither of us wanted me to move in with her! We both knew how difficult it was having my mother living with us years ago and had agreed way back then that we would not make that mistake. I remember her saying, "Mom, when you get old and I ask you to move in with me, do you promise to say no?" And besides, I needed my own place and space. Along my travel odyssey, I had made peace with the fact that I require a lot of alone time. I am basically an introvert with the occasional extroverted moments. But extrovert times needed to be balanced with reading, chanting, and meditating. I can happily make a day of such activities. If I stock up on food and do not have to set foot outside my door, all the better. This is hard to do when other people are around, requiring time and attention.

Nevertheless, I didn't want to be too far away from her and the baby. I knew California was too far away from Pennsylvania and my daughter and grandchild for it to be my permanent residence, but I needed to go to California soon to fetch Murphy, before his sitter moved. Once I got him, would I rent somewhere in California for a while? What about getting Murphy back to the East Coast? It's a long direct flight coast to coast, and he got really sick on the plane when we flew from Virginia to California. How was I going to get him back there? Would I fly halfway and stop a few days in a hotel and then continue? Getting a dog on a flight and through security isn't easy, and stopping and doing it twice seemed daunting.

As you can see, there were a lot of confusing thoughts and emotions surrounding the decision of where to put down roots for Murphy and me. When my mind wasn't busy wrestling with where to live and how to get there, it was trying to figure out how to write a book about grief and loss. I found myself doing research on grief for hours, and when I came upon something I wasn't familiar with, I felt anxious. I felt I had to read everything on the subject so I could be an expert! I was totally in my head researching and looking for writing courses and trying to figure it all out.

After a few years of assistant teaching with the Four Winds, I was asked to teach an online class. I had to learn quickly how to fluidly operate in the unfamiliar venue of virtual workplace. I learned about apps to test Wi-Fi strength so I could hold class anywhere I happened to be. I also created a shaman practice using Skype, FaceTime, and Zoom. Virtual work was new to me, but I went for it with full force, even though it sometimes felt as though my brain was spinning inside my head. One day I forwarded my daughter a memo I had prepared, listing the Wi-Fi requirements for supporting the Zoom platform we used for my online class. My daughter wrote back, "Who are you and what have you done with my mother who can't even figure out the TV remote?" If I could do all of that, maybe I could figure out how to write my book!

I picked up Murphy and rented an Airbnb in California for a month to figure things out. After trying to use all my creative problem-solving skills to analyze where to put down roots and how to write a book, I was stumped. All I had were a few paragraphs cobbled together and a healthy skepticism of my ability to navigate the publishing industry, which felt like an impenetrable wall. I felt like a failure. How was I going to explain to people that I couldn't figure out how to write a book? I had been a lawyer and a judge and yet the book-writing process seemed so complicated that I wasn't sure I really wanted to write one. And what about finding a place for Murphy and me to live? Everything seemed hopeless. I was at an impasse.

After one particularly frustrating day, Murphy and I went out to walk on the beach and watch the sunset; I got a familiar feeling I hadn't had for a while. It seemed I was observing myself watching the sunset. I realized I had been forgetting to get in touch with my Observer Within. My morning routine of sacred chanting had fallen away without my noticing. I had forgotten the practice of gratitude. I had become consumed by my anxiety-ridden thoughts and emotions, and they had completely hijacked my time and attention, and they were on the verge of squashing my dreams.

I had forgotten about making a daily practice of choosing joy and gratitude. The practice I held dear of living consequently every moment of every day had slipped away. It occurred to me with some amusement how easily I lost my focus to spend a lot of time worrying about the publishing details of a book I hadn't written because I was so worried about getting it published. And I was stressed out about where to live on the East Coast while stagnating on the West Coast. I had forgotten to concentrate on my wildest hopes and dreams and feel the wonder and excitement of a future living and experiencing those dreams.

I returned to my daily practice and regained my ability to watch my thoughts and emotions from a distance and then slow down, eventually stopping the process of trying to figure things out in my head. Instead I chanted and experienced the joy and gratitude I would feel when I finished my book and was living my passion of writing and talking to people about the journey with grief. I then prayed and felt in my whole being the joy and gratitude I would feel with Murphy in our new home and community. As I prayed and chanted, I became reacquainted with gratitude and joy and my essential self and my dreams.

I didn't have to read every single book written about grief to offer my wisdom. I would write a book about my own grief and my own journey of finding a new life filled with joy, hope, and grace. I didn't have to run to the East Coast and look for a place to live. In my mind the book had been written and the perfect place to live had been found, and I felt only the excitement of both achievements running through me as I left the details to be worked out in divine time.

I always remember my own instinctual knowledge of what is best and right for me, an instinct that has been growing within me and is becoming stronger since I became a crone and grandmother. I remember how I have always been drawn to chanting over meditation when it seemed that everyone around me was insisting on meditation as the way to enlightenment. I got something wonderful out of short meditation, but lengthy meditation never worked for me. I just couldn't relate. Sometimes snarky comments were made about the brevity of my attention span and I would try again, but it felt off.

Then I read a book by Perdita Finn, co-author of *The Way of the Rose: The Radical Path of the Divine Feminine Hidden in the Rosary*, referring to what she calls "macho male meditation practices." In her view meditation evolved from the hunting practices of men and the need for absolute stillness. Women, on the other hand, were gatherers, storytellers, and spell keepers. Finn also searched for enlightenment through meditation but found "how utterly her aspirations had been co-opted by patriarchal spiritual delusions that privileged silence over storytelling, the mind over the heart, celibacy over fertility, enlightenment over the healing wisdom of the darkness."

She turned instead to praying the 108 beads of the rosary to align herself with "old grannies, dismissed, overlooked, forgotten," who "hid their devotion to the Great Mother, the Great Granny, in those beads" even as the "patriarchal priesthood" told them to "Shut the f*#k up." Her words were both encouraging and soothing, allowing me to turn away from the rigors of meditation toward what felt natural to me, chanting with a string of 108 mala beads to focus my mind and to count mantras in sets of 108 repetitions.

I knew I had found my sacred path and a kinship with Catholic grandmothers praying the rosary with 108 beads and with Muslim grandmothers praying with the 100 beads of the misbaha. I also love the smooth and soothing feel of beads in my hand as I pray. The sound and vibration of chanting, like saying the rosary or other iterative prayers, stimulates the vagus nerve so I can sit quietly in a state of grace and remember to practice gratitude. As said so eloquently by Finn, "I don't want to be the Dalai Lama. I want to be my grandmother." Even more importantly, I aspire to be my authentic self. I just needed to remember that I am the only one who knows my own heart and what is best for me.

Once I returned to praying and chanting, things began to clear. I knew exactly where to go on the East Coast: my daughter wanted me near her, and even though Airbnb accommodations were limited in the area, one popped up immediately that I could rent for a month. I stopped researching and began writing my own book and telling my own transformation story. As I chanted and prayed, my mind calmed and I received the details I needed to structure my book. The words *as above, so below* came to me. Also the words *transcendence, resurrection,* and *rebirth.* These words guided my writing and became the special hero's journey of the bereaved mirroring the passage of our loved ones. Did these words come from my Observer Within, the collective consciousness, or from Spirit? I don't know for sure, but they came as I returned to practices dear to me. Instead of living in my head trying to figure things out, I was living in the joy and gratitude of my dreams—finishing my book and living near my daughter.

All I know for sure is being consumed by anxiety-ridden thoughts and fears took me too far away from the place of no mind. Finding my way back to my Observer Within allowed me to detach from my thoughts and emotions and to become open and available to receive the details I needed to complete my book and find a home. I had to dig deep and find my inner crone and grandmother energy, the energy that makes me uniquely and authentically me, the place from where I act with my inner wisdom to have become a sage.

NO TIME

Time only as a measure of past, present, and future is a functional necessity. The layers of times that quicken us, excite and inspire us is a symphony of possibilities awaiting our curiosity and commitment to life. What if we changed the very icon of time in order to see the many dimensions, parallel worlds, imaginal possibilities, and different types of time that surround us?

— Dr. Jean Houston

The practice of no time is seeing time as an infinite loop, bending backward and forward, rather than a straight arrow. It's a practice of stepping outside of ordinary time into sacred time, where the future and past reach out to inform present events. When we see time as an infinite loop, we learn to look for synchronicities, or the serendipitous occurrence of events, to guide us. Before Death Day/After Death Day—sometimes life seems irrevocably divided into before this and after that. Could I reawaken to excitement and inspiration and possibility?

What is synchronicity? *Synchronicity* is a concept first introduced by analytical psychologist Carl Jung, who defined it as an "acausal connecting principle" or a "meaningful coincidence." Jung's belief was that events may be connected by meaning and that they cannot be explained by causality. Causality comes from cause and effect: "I did X and then Y happened." Synchronicity comes from chance occurrences. It is the creative force of the universe working with you in this divine play we are living.

Synchronicity has also been referred to as the observation of omens. The wind blowing gently where it was still. The appearance of a magnificent animal in your path. It can be as simple as meeting the right person at the right time with the right information. Synchronicity can also be things lining up for you in unexpected ways—opening doors you never dreamed of or closing doors unexpectedly—that in hindsight you realize led you exactly where you needed to go.

Even if we don't know it, we shape-shift between the layers of time every day. Long ago I wanted to travel, and here I am. Long ago I made an eight-sided star that was perfect for my vision quest quilt 30 years later. Long ago I played as a child with a being that appeared to me as a fairy with beautiful wings, living in a tree in my backyard, invisible to anyone but me. And I lived in a house with a being in my basement that appeared to be Native American that only I could see. I now see these events as examples of time weaving back and forth in an infinite loop preparing me for who I am today and who I am becoming.

I know the dreams I launch into the future will return to me as synchronicities that I will follow forward like a path of magical breadcrumbs. Synchronicities stopped my frenetic traveling by having the wheels break on three of my suitcases to get my attention.

I wondered what other synchronicities would cross my path. After spending a few months in California, it was time to go to the East Coast to be there when my daughter's baby arrived. I hadn't purchased airline tickets because I was concerned about the complications of flying with Murphy. I also had a car in California that I would have to arrange to ship to Pennsylvania. I could solve both problems by driving cross-country, but I had never done it before and I was reluctant to drive alone.

One morning I got the idea of calling an old friend living in LA to get her opinion. Unknown to me, she was also planning a trip to Pennsylvania and did not want to fly there. The night before I called, she dreamed she would be traveling cross-country in a train or a car. She woke up feeling like the dream was an omen. And then I called! It turned out that we both wanted to leave immediately! She had driven cross-country several times before and felt comfortable, and I felt comfortable driving with her. Synchronicity dropped a solution into our laps!

Five days later, after shipping boxes and loading my car, getting directions and planning hotel stops, we were on our way. As we were at a filling station on the California state line, I got a call from the husband of a dear friend and former student. She was dying of cancer, and she had asked me months before whether I would go to Colorado when her time came and perform death rites for her. Shamanic death rites involve calling in guides and angels, opening chakras, and guiding the deceased through the portal to the upper world. It is a special privilege, and I felt honored that she had asked me.

I'd known she wasn't doing well, and when her husband called, he told me that she didn't have longer than a day or so and asked me to come immediately. My road-trip friend, also a shaman and a craniosacral worker, agreed to go with me. My friend and I sat at the station, canceling our hotel reservations and rerouting ourselves to go straight to Colorado. As we drove down the road, my friend pointed out that half a mile from the gas station, we would have turned right to go on our original route east, taking us away from Colorado. Once again, synchronicity was lining things up perfectly for my dying friend, and for us too.

We arrived in Colorado about 3:00 in the afternoon. I had a meaningful and intense discussion with my dying friend. We stared into each other eye's for a very long time, and she told me she wasn't ready to go. I assured her that I would stay in Colorado with her until she was ready. She continued to look deeply into my eyes, and I told her she wouldn't be alone for a moment; I would accompany her spirit all the way to the portal. That seemed to bring her peace, and just after midnight my dear friend passed. As I performed the death rites, the friend I was traveling with monitored my dead friend's craniosacral rhythms, which continue for some time after death. When the rites were complete, her craniosacral rhythm stopped completely, a confirmation that her soul had left and found its way home.

My friend had a green funeral, meaning she would be laid out at home and buried on property she and her husband owned in a shroud, not a coffin, under a tree that would be nurtured by her body. She was attended to after passing by a death doula who, in hospice, had monitored her for months. The green funeral director was also at her side. Dying around midnight meant that her five children were asleep, a blessing that gave us time to prepare her body before they woke up. While my driving friend attended to the grieving husband with craniosacral techniques, the three of us—death doula, funeral director, and shaman—attended to my friend's body.

I knew that this was another gift from my friend, allowing me to not only perform death rites but also giving me this special insight into how loving and caring an at-home death and funeral could be. Our loving hands washed every inch of her body, something that was too painful for her to endure at the end of her life when she couldn't bear to be touched. Then we anointed her with fragrant oils and dressed her in the last clothes she would ever wear, chosen by her husband. We washed and styled her hair, laid her out on her living room couch and surrounded her with flowers and colorful shawls. She had always had a bohemian spirit, and she was laid to rest dressed in colorful clothing, surrounded by color. She looked beautiful and peaceful when her children awoke and came downstairs. Synchronicity at work.

My friend and I left that morning, allowing the family to grieve. Murphy was an angel the entire time, playing with the kids and staying out of the way. We both knew all had participated in a sacred sacrament that had been perfectly orchestrated, even to the very detail of having my friend to drive along with me and having her skills in craniosacral work available for my friend's husband. We drove a long way that day in absolute silence. We both knew we had been shown something sacred, an at-home death and viewing.

We made it cross-country with perfect timing. My daughter and I were thrilled to be together during this special time and we had great fun together, shopping for the baby and the nursery as we waited for him to arrive. While waiting, I had time to consider where I might put down roots. I looked up properties on Zillow to see what was available near her but nothing appealed to me, and I couldn't shake the feeling that it would be a mistake to buy something. I didn't want to be a burden to my daughter by finding myself to be lonely and bored without a community of friends and acquaintances who were spiritually inclined.

The place that appealed to me spiritually was a small town on a lake in upstate New York, about three hours away from my daughter, where a shaman friend and Lakota pipe carrier lived. I had visited her lovely lake home many times over the past few years and felt drawn to the lake and to the community of strong, spiritual women. But I hadn't been able to find anything there in my price range.

When my daughter called to say her water broke and she was on her way to the hospital, I felt a sudden urge to spend the time waiting for the baby to come by looking for properties in New York. She only wanted her husband in the labor and delivery suite, so I opened up my laptop and started researching Zillow. I knew from looking previously that most places near the lake were either seasonal camps or million-dollar properties that were beyond my budget.

The problem with the seasonal homes was that a lot of time and money was required to turn them into year-round homes. I didn't have the time to take on a lengthy renovation —I needed a place to live. When I opened the page of listings on Zillow, a new one popped out at me. It was a newer home built in 2007, and although it wasn't directly on the lake, it had lake access and a seasonal view. I wondered as I looked at the listing why the picture of that home was so much larger than the others on the page.

The price was right, and the location was right. I would be a few hours away from my daughter—near enough to visit often and be available when she needed me, and far enough away not to be a burden. I loved the community of women I had met through my friend over the years, and I looked forward to being part of it. It just felt right. As my daughter was birthing her baby, I was birthing a home, ending up buying it sight unseen. Once my offer on the home was accepted, I went back to look again at the listing and download some of the pictures. I was surprised, but not shocked, to see that the picture in the listing that had appeared to be larger than the others was now the same size as all the others. I knew this was another synchronicity guiding me to the perfect house in perfect divine time.

Synchronicities are such powerful guidance that it has become a practice of observing the world around me for information. Often the numbers on my clock line up in perfect synchronicity, like 1:11 or 2:22, and I ask myself, *What am I considering at this moment?* It often seems the numbers align to indicate agreement with my plans. Agreement from whom? I believe it's my Observer Within, guides, angels, and those looking out for me. It was no surprise to me that as my grandson was coming into this world, synchronicity came to play in also birthing a home for me close by. It felt right and the timing was magical. My grandson's birthday is May 23rd and my home was purchased that day. As I looked into his sweet sleeping face, and at the beautiful face of his mother, my daughter, I knew we all are lovingly held together in the synchronicity of birthing.

All I know for sure is that looking for synchronicities affirms for me that my life is unfolding in perfect divine timing. As I reflect upon the mystery of time in all its infinite glory and all the myriad ways that past, present, and future ebb and flow and inform the precious present moment, I see how the universe conspires on my behalf and provides synchronicities to guide me.

I recently turned 66 and thought, *Wow! That seems like it might be a powerful number with some meaning for me.* The number 66 is an iterative number, repeating the number 6. It's an angel number carrying a message of abundance, optimism, and creativity. I took it as a sign of angels holding me in love and healing; a year promising to abound with synchronicities.

OWNING YOUR OWN PROJECTIONS

Our deepest fear is not that we are inadequate. Our deepest fear is that we are powerful beyond measure. It is our light, not our darkness, that most frightens us. We ask ourselves, who am I to be brilliant, gorgeous, talented, fabulous? Actually, who are you not to be?

— MARIANNE WILLIAMSON

To own your own projections, you must face all aspects of your personality, including the ones you don't like and wish to hide and the ones you do like but make you uncomfortable. Sometimes we can only see parts of ourselves in others because they are so deeply hidden in our own psyches. When you look at someone and say, "I don't like her because . . .," you are really saying you don't like that in yourself. When you look at someone and say, "Wow, I wish I could be like that . . .," you are likewise saying you like that quality in yourself. Jung calls our hidden parts "our shadows."

Finding and embracing our shadow parts, the good and the bad, keeps us from projecting them onto others and making them responsible for our pain or happiness. When we are fully integrated and aware, we see that we alone are responsible for all we create. When we make another person responsible for our pain or happiness, we assume the role of victim in that relationship. When we assume the role of victim, someone will step forward to fill the roles of perpetrator and rescuer. This creates what is called a triangle of disempowering roles. These roles continue in an unconscious fashion by everyone in the triangle until someone steps out of their chosen role, takes responsibility for themselves, and refuses to play the game.

I know that I am made up of all the parts of me. The failures and the successes, the pain and the joy, the brilliance and the absentmindedness. Even the annoyed and the short-tempered parts and the part that avoids emotions by reading. Because just as surely as I am capable of being surly and annoyed and avoidant, I am also capable of great and profound love and connection. I know that all of these parts make me who I am. It has taken a surprisingly long time for me to embrace that particular point.

I surely could have been a better daughter, wife, mother, and employee, but my failure stories no longer define me, and my success stories don't either. And I am working on no longer carrying and being triggered by the stories about what others have done to me and what I did to others. I realize that no one is to blame for my pain or happiness. It took a while for me to accept that Ben didn't die to cause me pain; he was ready to go, and it had nothing at all to do with me or anyone else. All the shame, blame, and guilt I carried around for so long were my own pain and feelings of worthlessness that I couldn't face.

If our perception of reality is based on all of our beliefs, even the ones we don't want to see, the ones hidden in our shadow, the light and the dark ones, then who are we when death comes on its wild, red-eyed stallion and tramples all of our beliefs into the dirt? Death changes everything.

The time of Ben's death was when I was most vulnerable and therefore most capable of change. I found myself outside of my life, looking in at . . . what? Habits and priorities of a lifetime based on my awe and admiration of the capabilities, attributes, and achievements of successful people I admired. I was in awe of them and tried to emulate them and their lifestyles. I wanted what they had; I wanted to be like them. But death came and exposed these projections. I suddenly saw behind the societal masks, and I felt disillusioned, tricked, and betrayed. But I found in myself awe and admiration for successful people who wanted to achieve success at any price.

I just didn't see it in myself until Ben passed. Because there was always someone richer, better educated, or more connected to powerful people, it was easy to see myself as still striving to catch up. No matter how much success I achieved, I always wondered, *What next?* When Ben passed, I began to ask why and how instead of what next. *Why had I made those choices along the way and how might things have turned out differently?*

I floundered around trying to find someone to blame so I could abandon my personal responsibility for the life I created. I wanted to be a victim. I felt like a victim. How had this happened to me? To my family? I felt ashamed and disgraced and singled out. I was angry, and I wanted revenge. I blamed everyone and everything around me: the police for not stopping the drugs, the dealer for selling the drugs, Ben's friends for not watching out for him, his father for not being around enough, and the list went on and on. I blamed myself too. I looked back at every decision I had ever made and wondered what would have happened if I had chosen the other fork in the road when he was young, and when I still believed I had control.

I can tell you that those obsessive thoughts led to madness. I spent long hours lying on Ben's bed ruminating and tossing and turning. Projecting all my pain onto others did not help at all. Rather, I lost myself more, and the loss went deeper and deeper the more I chose blame as my coping mechanism and victimhood as my badge of honor. I was now a member of an elite group of grieving mothers. I could have chosen to stay in that group forever and embody that heavy role, allowing it to define my life and my choices.

Even after I fled my home and job and all that was familiar to me, I carried that victimhood along with me. I was at a crossroads in my life. I thought I could leave my pain and blame behind, but instead, the longer I was away from all that was familiar, the more I had to face the truth. What I really was struggling to find were answers to my soul's journey here on earth.

In the stillness of the mountains and deserts and the timeless quiet of temples, I became aware of something new inside me. I found peace, in the quiet my mind became tranquil, and in my search of sacred places, I found the sacred within me.

In time, I was able to connect with my inner self as well as to the loss of my center after Ben's death. In time, I was able to connect with my inner self, my essential self, that I lost after Ben's death. But it was a process of recovering pieces of my soul connected to loss of self-worth, self-guidance, and self-reliance. Even in my travels I sought out people and situations that confirmed my self-selected victim role. It felt comfortable to be around people who would continue in the role of perpetrator and bully me and remind me that I was simply not good enough—never had been and never would be—until one day it was no longer comfortable.

Ben's death had resulted in a complete deconstruction of my reality, I could not relate to my old life and fled, leaving everything behind. What I didn't realize was how desperately I was looking for terra firma, solid ground, under my feet. Not only was I in search of a way to understand grief and honor my son, I was also looking for love and acceptance to soothe and support my quest. While the search for ways to work with my profound grief took me all over the world and brought me to the shamanic path, I see now that my grief was so overwhelming that my search for love and acceptance played out in the background in a very negative way.

Desperately seeking love and acceptance, I was vulnerable and grabbed on to whoever came along. When I was promised love and community, I totally bought in. I closed my eyes to any behaviors I found disturbing or disempowering. I used to wonder why I was treated differently, with less respect and more condescending behavior, until one day I couldn't ignore it anymore. I had an aha moment, where I saw clearly the roles we all were playing and realized I had been keeping my head in the sand and overlooking or justifying behaviors I could no longer tolerate. I remember a feeling of waking up and seeing clearly what I had been working so hard to avoid.

I saw with open eyes how my fear of being rejected, abandoned, and forlorn, alone with my grief, had manifested in extreme acts of people-pleasing and not sharing my truth—in short, victimhood. The thing about people-pleasing is that you can never dance fast enough or jump high enough to please someone who has taken on the role of the perpetrator, the unpleasable one. The dance between a victim and perpetrator can only become more and more intense until and unless one of the dancers stops—and walks away.

The day I became cognizant of how my victim role brought out the perpetrator in others, I shed the role. I took responsibility with loving kindness to myself for my fears of being rejected, abandoned, and forlorn. I saw how my desperate need for terra firma, love, and acceptance after Ben's death brought out the bully, the perpetrator, in those I chose to be around. Once I saw my part, I saw through the reality of the circumstances to the illusionary aspect of life.

Even so, I still found myself on the horns of a dilemma. Could I give up this victim role? Could I accept all the changes stepping out would bring? Instead of lashing out in anger and resentment to protect my wounded ego, could I evolve past that response? I knew this was a defining moment. I clearly saw that I had carried the role of victim all my life. From my beginnings, I carried the wound of never pleasing my parents, and it caused me to always try to please others. I would try to turn myself into whatever they wanted me to be, trying to find love and acceptance and prove my worth, while at the same time rejecting the ones who did love and accept me because in my twisted way of thinking, they clearly didn't know much.

I knew that how I chose to react in this moment had the potential to change everything. I always thought of myself as an empowered woman because I equated success with empowerment. But success did not make me emotionally whole; it was a facade I used to hide my insecurities, much like the wizard of Oz hid his frailties behind a curtain while projecting a big and powerful image to the world: "Pay no attention to the man behind the curtain," the wizard yells in vain. He was discovered and seen for who he really was. Once I saw my victim role and how it created the movie of my life, it put everything in perspective. It was easy to forgive the bullies and the rescuers when I saw my victimhood as my life's work to heal. It was not a struggle to choose evolution, or in the vernacular of the East, rebirth.

Not only did I have to give up my victim role, but I also had to give up my own bully role. There were family members whom I blamed for not helping Ben. There were those who did not step up to meet with him and talk with him. There were those whom I felt had abandoned him. I stopped speaking to them and cut them out of my life. I felt punishing them was justified until I saw that this, too, was holding me back. Once I saw my behavior as that of a bully or perpetrator, I realized it was keeping me in the triangle of disempowering relationships. It was surprisingly difficult to let that role go because these people had wronged my son. But letting go of my anger and resentment was another choice for my personal evolution. For rebirth.

I believe that finding the sacred inside myself and turning 66, a ripe old age by any measure, brought in the energy of the crone and the grandmother. Crone energy felt different, and I felt different. I felt less and less like a victim and more and more like a no-bullshit elder. I looked at my dyed-blonde hair and suddenly it didn't fit anymore. I decided to let it grow out into its natural, mostly white color. How many years had I been dyeing my hair blonde? As many years as I had been going through life in the role of the victim.

In my new house, in my new community, I now strive to be authentic. Rather than trying hard to be pleasing to find love and acceptance, I find both by being myself. I recently heard myself repeating an old story about how I was like a golden retriever, always trying to make everyone a friend. As I heard myself retelling that old analogy, I stopped and created a new ending: "But no more. Now I allow those who like me to come and those who don't to go." Changing the ending was extremely freeing.

My dear shaman and pipe-carrying friend and I end each invitation to each other to go somewhere or do something with the word *freedom!* In other words we are reminding each other that we always have the freedom to choose whether we want to go. And we have the freedom to change our minds at the last minute. No hard feelings and no questions asked. We accept each other as we are—no pretensions, only authenticity.

I joined a group of hers, women who meet to discuss the channeled literature of Paul Selig, who receives clairaudient dictation from unseen intellects called the Guides. In *The Book of Freedom*, Selig shows readers how to fully express their divine self by surrendering to the true nature of their being. Our divine selves, or what I call the Observer Within, wants us to be free of the triangle of disempowerment and stand fully awake and alive as our authentic selves.

As I awakened fully to the power of freedom to be myself, I created a Power of 8 healing group based on the book by Lynne McTaggert. The group decided to meet on the same day as the book group. I decided to leave the book group and continue with the Power of 8 group instead. The old me would have been too afraid to alienate my friends. The new me knew that I was free to change my mind and to live the life I wanted.

As I shed the role of victim and rearranged how I engaged with those around me, I no longer attracted bullies who loved finding a victim to torment. I also no longer attracted rescuers who loved finding a victim to manipulate or felt the need to bully anyone. I was just me, cautiously forging new relationships, making choices that pleased myself, and refusing to re-create any aspect of the triangle of disempowerment with anyone. I began to be able to appreciate my own light, which I hadn't been able to see through the smoky lens of my victimhood. I refuse to play small for anyone and I know my own worth.

All I know for sure is that seeing and disowning my victim role allowed me to release my fears of being rejected, abandoned, and forlorn. I no longer feel the need to be pleasing to find love and acceptance; I find both by being authentically me. I no longer allow myself to be treated as less than deserving of respect. I was ready to find a loving community of acceptance, I was ready to love all parts of me, and I was ready for rebirth. Releasing the perpetrator, the bully in me, allowed me to let go of my anger and resentment. The crone energy came to prepare me to become the best grandmother possible to my grandson, this new life that landed on planet Earth. I was a no-bullshit, kick-ass survivor of a grandmother! I was prepared for my personal evolution, for rebirth.

INDIGENOUS ALCHEMY

The Mystical Shaman dances between worlds, wearing the cloak of the world loosely around his shoulders, and sings the world into being. He reminds us to be in the world and travel through it, but not to be defined by it or become too attached to the experience. This is the symbol of true alchemy, for all elements of life have a spiritual aspect and a material one. When we remember this, all manner of miracles and manifestations are possible.

— MYSTICAL SHAMAN ORACLE DECK BY ALBERTO VILLOLDO, PH.D., COLETTE BARON-REID, AND MARCELA LOBOS

You might be wondering, What the heck does "indigenous alchemy" mean? For *indigenous*, I like the dictionary definition of "something innate, inherent, and natural to humans, like feelings." For *alchemy*, I like the definition "transformation of matter." So maybe it means "an innate desire for transformation." Or perhaps, to put it in quantum physics terms, "the transformation from particles to waves and back, depending upon whether or not we are looking." It is natural for us to desire transformation, not for us to remain stuck.

Quantum physics has several really cool concepts. One is "delayed choice," or the quantum eraser. The experiment shows that when photons, electrons, or any atomic-size objects are shot toward a screen with two slits, an "interference pattern" emerges and they begin to act like waves. The single piece of matter becomes a "wave" of potentials, expressing itself in the form of multiple possibilities. This matter exists and expresses itself in multiple states until it is "measured" or "observed." When observed the piece of matter collapses into one single path. It's as if the particle knows it's being watched. The observer has some sort of effect on the behavior of the particle. This is called quantum uncertainty.

Indigenous alchemy is a call to action whenever we get too comfortable or complacent in our lives. As I completed my journey around the practices of the medicine wheel, I was in the throes of new beginnings. It turns out that this newly minted crone finds herself to be a very contrary and empowered woman. I find myself aiming the word *disempowering* at a lot of situations that just don't feel right to me anymore. And then I find myself dreaming and sending arrows of empowering newness into the future.

I'm now listening closely to the elements of the old stories I used to tell myself and replacing them with new and empowered stories. I know that replacing the old with the new will result in the expression of new possibilities. Routines are like projections in that they keep you at a low frequency. I am choosing change so I can continue to grow. As I let go of everything holding me back from my full potential,

I begin to celebrate what is. All the pretending and performing has to go—all the coping mechanisms to protect myself from feeling inadequate and getting hurt.

Despite my coping mechanisms, I did get hurt, and none of my habitual contrivances saved me from pain. I still get hurt and I still get my heart broken, but I welcome the pain because it shows me where I'm stuck and where I have more healing to do. I don't go back to the illusion of safety in sameness anymore. I know that going forward and creating new possibilities is what my soul longs for. Have you heard the saying "A foolish consistency is the hobgoblin of little minds"? This remark comes from the essay "Self-Reliance" by Ralph Waldo Emerson. I love it. The concept of "foolish consistency" resonates with me. There is no safety in consistency and no badge of honor for staying stuck. All we get from that is putting a period at the end of the rest of your sentence on planet Earth.

I don't want to live my life like it's a life sentence. I almost did—I almost lived a life of leaving Ben's room a shrine and turning my home into my prison. But Ben saved me—he showed me the way out. Ben didn't want a shrine, and he didn't want me to be in a prison of mourning. He wants me to live. He's happy that I'm happy. It was part of his mission and he gets an A-plus-plus. I'm proud of him and all he accomplished on planet Earth and all he is contributing on the other side. The hermetic tradition teaches us as above, so below; as within, so without. Ben is a shining testament to that. Our journey of grief is a testament to that. Our loved ones—and we too—have their very own hero's odyssey through transition, resurrection, and rebirth.

As for me, my journey brought me to the closure of writing this book, the beginnings of developing a course around living with grief, and a growing shaman practice helping grieving people and their loved ones. One of the concepts of a hero's quest is returning with gifts. At the beginning of my journey, I retired from my judicial position and later burned my judicial robes in the vision quest fire. When I retired, I did not anticipate ever practicing law again. When I burned my judicial robes, I was closing doors, symbolically demonstrating my intent to release the past.

In my new community, I see the need for lawyers willing to work with juveniles and provide legal services to people who can't afford big-firm prices. There are advocacy and environmental groups of all kinds who operate on a shoestring budget and are in need of legal research. There's even a shortage of lawyers willing to do real estate closings in my area. I wondered whether going back into practice was a step forward or a step backward. As I sat meditating, after pulling out my prayer beads and chanting the Gāyatrī Mantra 108 times, I knew exactly what to do—reinstate my law license and use it to help people in need. I'm not going back to my old law practice or my old ways. I'm going forward, choosing to use my practice of law in a different way.

The Gāyatrī Mantra appeared in the Rig Veda, an early Vedic text written between 1800 and 1500 B.C.E. It is recognized in the Bhagavad Gita as the poem of the divine. It's an ancient, ecstatic poem of gratitude to the divine in all things.

The eternal earth, air, heaven
That glory, that resplendence of the sun
May we contemplate the brilliance of that
light. May the sun inspire our minds.

— Translation by Douglas Brooks, Ph.D., a professor of religion at the University of Rochester and a teacher in the Rajanaka yoga tradition

I was talking over my plan to reinstate my law license with a Lakota elder who was 85 years old and full of wisdom. She said, "What you didn't see that we all did was that you were already a shaman before you ever started your training." In indigenous cultures, the shamans are those who were recognized as leaders in their community. She told me that no one but me ever doubted my leadership and that I was a shaman. I just needed to spiral around the wheel a few times to see it for myself. She told me that as she watched me burn my robe in the vision quest fire, she knew I was burning up old ways of thinking. She said, "Of course you came back to the law and back to yourself. You came home."

All I know for sure is that I will continue to dream big dreams because I know that the future hasn't happened yet. It is still forming, and I am still choosing outcomes—even ones that incorporate the stars and galaxies, that save the planet and bring world peace. Too much? I don't think so—physicists have recently observed a giant magnetic bridge between us and our closest galactic neighbors, the Large Magellanic Cloud and Small Magellanic Cloud. The bridge is called the Magellanic Bridge. The bridge was found by a research team at the University of Sydney in Australia, and reported by the Resonance Science Foundation headed by Nassim Haramein, a brilliant quantum physicist. I plan to walk across that bridge to the stars and galaxies and beyond.

Now I understand the message of light that came through me when I stood on a sacred beach with my medicine stones. Now I understand how to live the rest of my life. In the words of Elise de Wolfe, "I'm going to make everything around me more beautiful—that will be my life."

Exercises to Apply the Practices of the
East Direction of the Medicine Wheel
and Bring Rebirth to Your Life

We are nearing the end of our journey together—and individually.

Just as you did with the previous exercises, begin by finding a notebook, a pen or pencil, a candle, and a small tin pie pan or tray. The pan will be used to catch ashes later in the exercise. In this exercise, you will write honest answers to four questions, then set an intent, hold them to the candle flame, and burn them. By burning them you release them to your concept of God, or Spirit, or Universe for your healing. Then allow your heart to open to allow in new ways of filling the newly emptied space.

If you would rather light a fire in your fireplace or outside, that's fine too. In shamanic mythology, fire is a path of rapid transformation, so by burning your answers, you allow rapid transformation into your life. There's no need to worry that someone might find your answers because you will be burning them. This will allow you to be completely and radically honest in your answers because no one will see them but you.

Next find somewhere you can sit alone in stillness with your notebook, pen or pencil, candle, and pie pan beside you. Allow yourself this alone time when you have nowhere to go and nothing to do. As you sit concentrate on your in-breath and your out-breath. When we breathe, we empty our lungs of old, stale air so fresh, new air can come in. Our breath is a metaphor for the exercises in this book. We are in the process of breathing out old, stale ways of being so new ones have space to live inside us. In solitude we can hear the voices inside ourselves that grow faint and are drowned out by the noise and busyness of our daily lives and by the presence of other people. Stay still until you are in a place of knowing that what you are hearing is the subtle voice of your spirit. Stay until the doors and walls you have erected around your broken heart are open. Once you feel ready, ask yourself the questions below and answer with radical honesty. That means no holds barred, nothing held back, courageously naming that which must be named for your transformation.

Ask yourself each of the following questions one at a time and then immediately take your answers to the fire before moving on to the next question.

By now you are familiar with sitting alone in stillness and finding the subtle voice of your spirit. You may be filled with thoughts and emotions that have arisen throughout this journey. Perhaps you are awash in many emotions, trying to sort out what to do next. Instead of thinking and sorting, sit and allow your Observer Within to just watch all those swirling thoughts and emotions. Watch them swirling just like the snow swirls when you shake a snow globe. Write down as many of the swirling thoughts and emotions as you can, and when you are finished, burn your list in your candle flame or in your fire with the intention of creating space for your own inner wisdom telling you what you need to do to go forward. Then open your heart to what your inner wisdom is telling you, or if you are still waiting on answers, just write a thank-you to your Observer Within in gratitude for always being there.

Take some time to look for synchronicities and make a list. Maybe you see a message on a license plate that confirms your wisdom. Maybe you see an image of your loved one or iterative numbers pop up just as you are wondering whether you are on the right track. Then burn your list in your candle flame or in your fire with the intention of releasing anything preventing you from seeing and believing synchronicities. Open your heart and allow yourself to be guided by synchronicities.

Consider the triangle of disempowerment. Are you being a victim? Are you being a perpetrator or rescuer? Make a list of all the roles you are playing in the triangle, and take them to your candle flame or fire and burn them with the intent to release them all so you are free of the triangle of disempowerment. Open your heart and allow yourself to no longer be disempowered or to disempower anyone else.

Make a list of any places in which you still feel stuck in complacency. List them and then burn that list with the intention of releasing them. Open your heart with the intention of allowing indigenous alchemy, your innate desire for transformation, to guide you.

CHAPTER SIX

Transcendence

After the Journey

*Try not to resist the changes that come your way. Instead
let life live through you. And do not worry that your life is
turning upside down. How do you know that the side
you are used to is better than the one to come?*

— RUMI

I miss Ben every single day. I miss having him here bopping his head and singing me silly songs. I miss his big presence and giving him a hug. I miss the grandchildren that he
might have shared with me. And yet I have a relationship
with him that is profoundly different from anything I could
have imagined. When someone asks me how many children I have, I used to just want to shrivel up and crawl away.
Now I just say two children, one daughter in physical form
and one son in spirit. Yes, I do get looks of shocked horror,
but now I'm okay with it. I've embraced it, and now we can
really talk about what's important in my life and in yours.

I can be that person who understands, and so can you.
We are ultimately all touched by death. So many people are
carrying hurt around and hiding the pain of the loss of a

sibling, or a niece, or a nephew, or a cousin, or a co-worker, or a friend, or a husband, or a mother, or a father. Or a child. So many people are hiding their experiences of seeing or hearing the person they have lost. So many people are hiding their grieving hearts because they have been told "It's time to move on" or "You have to get over it." I say I'll never get over it, but I have gotten through it.

Ben and I went on a journey together through transformation, resurrection, and rebirth, and we both came out on the other side profoundly changed. We would not have made this quest had Ben not died. I know that Ben pulled me and sometimes carried me through my journey. I know that his death was a gift of love to me and a catalyst for change. Thank you, dear Ben, for your life and for your death. The moment you came into my life, you were a precious miracle who gave me the grace to become a mother. The moment you left this life, you were an inspiration who gave me the grace to become what I am today: a shaman, a writer, a teacher, and a newly repurposed lawyer.

There's a wonderful book called *Walking Each Other Home* by Ram Dass and Mirabai Bush. I love the sweet and generous letters Ram Dass wrote to the bereaved parents of a son and daughter. I want to share the profound wisdom of Ram Dass, who recently passed. In one letter he talks about grieving and how "it will allow you and your son to know each other in another way, and that other way of knowing may give balance to the grief," and now that "his captivating form is no longer present, you are freer to make contact with his soul." In a second letter to parents grieving the loss of a daughter, Ram Dass says, "Something in you dies when you bear the unbearable, and it is only in that dark night of the soul that you are prepared to see as God sees and to love as God loves," and that their daughter "came through you to do her work on earth, which includes her manner of death."

These words sum up my experience and I hope they will speak to you as well, in the sense that we are able to continue our loving relationships beyond death, and this experience is transforming. It gives me much comfort to know that Ben came through me to do his work and that part of his work was the manner of his death. I believe that my role in his life was to support his work here on planet Earth, and I did that to the best of my ability. I wish I knew then what I know now because I would do many things differently. I would have worried less and loved more, knowing that part of my work here on earth was to simply support his. In the wise words of Maya Angelou, "When we know better, we do better."

I don't want to leave you with the impression that by doing all the exercises in this book, you will be free from grief. Not at all. We learn to live with grief and use its power to make changes for the better in our own lives so we can touch and heal others. The pain will always be with us, but we can release the despair, guilt, and anger that make our grief unbearable and that keep us stuck. November 2, 2019, was the fifth anniversary of Ben's death. It was a really big and difficult one for me and it rocked me to my core. At one point I was back to feeling that everyone around me were aliens and I could not seem to connect. It was painful to try to make conversation, and even holding someone's hand to say grace was unbearable. I wasn't prepared for it, even though I have done all the exercises and written this book.

I was almost embarrassed by the depth of my grieving. I felt like this grieving was too much and I should be doing better! I'm supposed to be an inspiration, but I could barely function. I was back to judging myself. Then it came to me that even this was given to me to pass along. Sometimes grief will hit us with another big wave of pain and we have to allow ourselves to feel the pain of our loss whenever it comes. The pain is real and it is part of the great love we feel. And then I looked at the pain and my feelings to see whether some of the stories about shame, blame, and guilt were rising up again. I noticed myself blaming myself, wondering again whether I, or others, could have saved him by doing things differently.

I needed to go back to the exercises because at the root of this deep grief was lingering guilt, anger, and self-judgment. Working my way through the 16 exercises, I found the places that were still raw and in need of healing, and I took them again to the fire for transformation. Only then could I return to a place of peace, understanding that even though I used the energy and wisdom of my grief to create a new and better life, I still miss Ben: my person, the one who is unique and special to me and who will always live in my heart.

One last time, I invite you to sit in your quiet spot, the one that is familiar to you by now, and light a candle with the intent to bring in the sacred to illuminate and inspire you while you are doing this last assignment.

Write your story—the one starring you in all your glory, the newly minted self you found on your journey with grief. Be sure to include the gifts you found along the way, and all the wisdom brought to you by death. Take your dreams into your heart for safekeeping. Treasure your story and revisit it every day as you are enfolded in the wings of Love.

May you be at peace. May your heart remain open. May you awaken to the light of your own true nature. May you be healed. May you be a source of healing for all beings.

— TIBETAN BUDDHIST PRAYER

Acknowledgments

I am so honored to be able to express my gratitude to those who are an integral part of my journey and who guided me and were my cheerleaders through this process. To my son Ben who taught me about life on earth and life after death. To my daughter Caty who held me up through the funeral arrangements, encouraged me to leave my home, my job and all that was familiar to become a homeless seeker of answers to the great question, "What is the meaning of grief?" To my son-in-law, Hans Otten, who opened up his basement to the boxes and bags I left behind for two and a half years and who allowed me to crash as needed. To my little grandson, Vaughn, and baby Anika whose love brings me home. To my little Westie dog, Murphy, who comforts and loves me every day.

I owe a great debt of gratitude to my Hay House editor, Melody Guy, who always has sound advice, who allowed my authentic voice to flow, and who led me, a brand-new author, through the publishing process seamlessly. I must also mention kn literary arts who helped me find a great editor, Annie Wylde, to help me with my initial drafts. I also want to express my gratitude to Hay House who encourages new authors, took a chance on me, and brought this book forward. And, so much love and gratitude to Joél Simone Anthony, mortician, author and teacher of *Sayin' It Louder: A Conversation about A Good Death in a Racist Society.* Thank you for becoming a dear friend and for reviewing my book for cultural sensitivity.

Every day I thank Elizabeth Lesser, founder of Omega institute and author of so many books, for taking a moment to respond to me, a woman she never met, when I was in the depths of despair and who continues to support and encourage me. Elizabeth, you may not know it but you saved my life that day. Thank you to Linda Star Wolf, a shaman sister whose work I love, who wrote the foreword to this book. I also want to thank Dr. Alberto Villoldo and Marcela Lobos for their continued guidance and support and all the staff and faculty of the Four Winds Society. You taught me well. And much love to all my students who allow me to walk the path of the shaman with them.

Finally, to all my "Besties." To Martina Von Rettig who traveled with me, befriended me, laughed uproariously with me, and held my soul in her mystical hands. To Nettie Jean Scarzafava; who opened her home to me to write non-stop for three weeks on her dining room table, and who continues to offer food and comfort. To the "lake ladies" who wrapped their loving arms around me. To Karen Peters who painstakingly edited my drafts. To Maria Fernandez who read and loved and supported. To Bobbie McCartney who advised and read and kept on reading. Thank you, Beloveds.

About the Author

Karen Johnson is a graduate of Georgetown Law Center (J.D.), a former Fulbright Scholar in Afghanistan, and holds master's megrees in public health and public and international affairs (MPH, MPIA). Karen is a retired federal administrative law judge who practiced criminal and energy law for more than 30 years. She also is a former U.S. Army officer, major, USAR (inactive).

Karen was personally trained by Alberto Villoldo and the Four Winds Society and holds a certification in Luminous Healing from Healing the Light Body School. She has trained extensively in the techniques of illumination, soul retrieval, extractions of energies and entities, divination, and death rites.

https://karenjohnson.net/

Hay House Titles of Related Interest

We hope you enjoyed this Hay House book. If you'd like to receive our online catalog featuring additional information on Hay House books and products, or if you'd like to find out more about the Hay Foundation, please contact:

Hay House, Inc., P.O. Box 5100, Carlsbad, CA 92018-5100
(760) 431-7695 or (800) 654-5126
(760) 431-6948 (fax) or (800) 650-5115 (fax)
www.hayhouse.com® • www.hayfoundation.org

Published in Australia by: Hay House Australia Pty. Ltd.,
18/36 Ralph St., Alexandria NSW 2015
Phone: 612-9669-4299 • *Fax:* 612-9669-4144
www.hayhouse.com.au

Published in the United Kingdom by: Hay House UK, Ltd.,
The Sixth Floor, Watson House, 54 Baker Street, London W1U 7BU
Phone: +44 (0)20 3927 7290 • *Fax:* +44 (0)20 3927 7291
www.hayhouse.co.uk

Published in India by: Hay House Publishers India,
Muskaan Complex, Plot No. 3, B-2, Vasant Kunj, New Delhi 110 070
Phone: 91-11-4176-1620 • *Fax:* 91-11-4176-1630
www.hayhouse.co.in

Access New Knowledge.
Anytime. Anywhere.

Learn and evolve at your own pace
with the world's leading experts.

www.hayhouseU.com